EDUCATION IN A COMPETITIVE AND GLOBALIZING WORLD SERIES

SEXUALITY EDUCATION

EDUCATION IN A COMPETITIVE AND GLOBALIZING WORLD SERIES

Success in Mathematics Education
Caroline B. Baumann
2009. ISBN: 978-1-60692-299-6

Mentoring: Program Development, Relationships and Outcomes
Michael I. Keel (Editor)
2009. ISBN: 978-1-60692-287-3

Mentoring: Program Development, Relationships and Outcomes
Michael I. Keel (Editor)
2009. ISBN: 978-1-60876-727-4 (Online Book)

Motivation in Education
Desmond H. Elsworth (Editor)
2009. ISBN: 978-1-60692-234-7

Evaluating Online Learning: Challenges and Strategies for Success
Arthur T. Weston (Editor)
2009. ISBN: 978-1-60741-107-9

Enhancing Prospects of Longer-Term Sustainability of Cross-Cultural INSET Initiatives in China
Chunmei Yan
2009. ISBN: 978-1-60741-615-9

Reading at Risk: A Survey of Literary Reading in America
Rainer D. Ivanov
2009. ISBN: 978-1-60692-582-9

Reading: Assessment, Comprehension and Teaching
Nancy H. Salas and Donna D. Peyton (Editors)
2009. ISBN: 978-1-60692-615-4

Reading: Assessment, Comprehension and Teaching
Nancy H. Salas and Donna D. Peyton (Editors)
2009. ISBN: 978-1-60876-543-0 (Online Book)

Multimedia in Education and Special Education
Onan Demir and Cari Celik
2009. ISBN: 978-1-60741-073-7

Rural Education in the 21st Century
Christine M.E. Frisiras (Editor)
2009. ISBN: 978-1-60692-966-7

Nutrition Education and Change
Beatra F. Realine (Editor)
2009. ISBN: 978-1-60692-983-4

The Reading Literacy of U.S. Fourth-Grade Students in an International Context
Justin Baer, Stéphane Baldi, Kaylin Ayotte, Patricia J. Gree and Daniel McGrath
2009. ISBN: 978-1-60741-138-3

Teacher Qualifications and Kindergartners' Achievements
Cassandra M. Guarino, Laura S. Hamilton, J.R. Lockwood, Amy H. Rathbun and Elvira Germino Hausken
2009. ISBN: 978-1-60741-180-2

PCK and Teaching Innovations
Syh-Jong Jang
2009. ISBN: 978-1-60741-147-5

IT- Based Project Change Management System
Faisal Manzoor Arain and Low Sui Pheng
2009. ISBN: 978-1-60741-148-2

Learning in the Network Society and the Digitized School
Rune Krumsvik (Editor)
2009. ISBN: 978-1-60741-172-7

Effects of Family Literacy Interventions on Children's Acquisition of Reading
Ana Carolina Pena (Editor)
2009. ISBN: 978-1-60741-236-6

Approaches to Early Childhood and Elementary Education
Francis Wardle
2009. ISBN: 978-1-60741-643-2

Academic Administration: A Quest for Better Management and Leadership in Higher Education
Sheying Chen (Editor)
2009. ISBN: 978-1-60741-732-3

Recent Trends in Education
Borislav Kuzmanović and Adelina Cuevas (Editors)
2009. ISBN: 978-1-60741-795-8

Expanding Teaching and Learning Horizons in Economic Education
Franklin G. Mixon, Jr. and Richard J. Cebula
2009. ISBN: 978-1-60741-971-6

New Research in Education: Adult, Medical and Vocational
Edmondo Balistrieri and Giustino DeNino (Editors)
2009. ISBN: 978-1-60741-873-3

Disadvantaged Students and Crisis in Faith-Based Urban Schools
Thomas G. Wilson
2010. ISBN: 978-1-60741-535-0

Delving into Diversity: An International Exploration of Issues of Diversity in Education
Vanessa Green and Sue Cherrington (Editors)
2010. ISBN: 978-1-60876-361-0

Developments in Higher Education
Mary Lee Albertson (Editor)
2010. ISBN: 978-1-60876-113-5

The Process of Change in Education: Moving from Descriptive to Prescriptive Research
Baruch Offir
2010. ISBN: 978-1-60741-451-3

Career Development
Hjalmar Ohlsson and Hanne Borg (Editors)
2010. ISBN: 978-1-60741-464-3

Adopting Blended Learning for Collaborative Work in Higher Education
Alan Hogarth
2010. ISBN: 978-1-60876-260-6

Special Education in the 21st Century
MaryAnn T. Burton (Editor)
2010. ISBN: 978-1-60741-556-5

Challenges of Quality Education in Sub-Saharan African Countries
Daniel Namusonge Sifuna and Nobuhide Sawamura
2010. ISBN: 978-1-60741-509-1

Collaborative Learning: Methodology, Types of Interactions and Techniques
Edda Luzzatto and Giordano DiMarco (Editors)
2010. ISBN: 978-1-60876-076-3

Handbook of Lifelong Learning Developments
Margaret P. Caltone (Editor)
2010. ISBN: 978-1-60876-177-7

Virtual Worlds: Controversies at the Frontier of Education
Kieron Sheehy, Rebecca Ferguson and Gill Clough (Editors)
2010. ISBN: 978-1-60876-261-3

Health Education: Challenges, Issues and Impact
André Fortier and Sophie Turcotte (Editors)
2010. ISBN: 978-1-60876-568-3

Reading in 2010: A Comprehensive Review of a Changing Field
Michael F. Shaughnessy (Editor)
2010. ISBN: 978-1-60876-659-8

Becoming an Innovative Teacher Educator: Designing and Developing a Successful Hybrid Course
Qiuyun Lin
2010. ISBN: 978-1-60876-465-5

Sexuality Education
Kelly N. Stanton (Editor)
2010. ISBN: 978-1-60692-153-1

EDUCATION IN A COMPETITIVE AND GLOBALIZING WORLD SERIES

SEXUALITY EDUCATION

KELLY N. STANTON
EDITOR

Nova Science Publishers, Inc.
New York

Copyright © 2010 by Nova Science Publishers, Inc.

All rights reserved. No part of this book may be reproduced, stored in a retrieval system or transmitted in any form or by any means: electronic, electrostatic, magnetic, tape, mechanical photocopying, recording or otherwise without the written permission of the Publisher.

For permission to use material from this book please contact us:
Telephone 631-231-7269; Fax 631-231-8175
Web Site: http://www.novapublishers.com

NOTICE TO THE READER

The Publisher has taken reasonable care in the preparation of this book, but makes no expressed or implied warranty of any kind and assumes no responsibility for any errors or omissions. No liability is assumed for incidental or consequential damages in connection with or arising out of information contained in this book. The Publisher shall not be liable for any special, consequential, or exemplary damages resulting, in whole or in part, from the readers' use of, or reliance upon, this material. Any parts of this book based on government reports are so indicated and copyright is claimed for those parts to the extent applicable to compilations of such works.

Independent verification should be sought for any data, advice or recommendations contained in this book. In addition, no responsibility is assumed by the publisher for any injury and/or damage to persons or property arising from any methods, products, instructions, ideas or otherwise contained in this publication.

This publication is designed to provide accurate and authoritative information with regard to the subject matter covered herein. It is sold with the clear understanding that the Publisher is not engaged in rendering legal or any other professional services. If legal or any other expert assistance is required, the services of a competent person should be sought. FROM A DECLARATION OF PARTICIPANTS JOINTLY ADOPTED BY A COMMITTEE OF THE AMERICAN BAR ASSOCIATION AND A COMMITTEE OF PUBLISHERS.

LIBRARY OF CONGRESS CATALOGING-IN-PUBLICATION DATA

Stanton, Kelly N.
  Sexuality education / Kelly N. Stanton.
       p. cm.
  Includes index.
  ISBN 978-1-60692-153-1 (softcover)
  1. Sex instruction--United States. 2. Teenagers--Sexual behavior--United States. 3. Teenage pregnancy--United States. I. Title.
  HQ57.5.A3S74 2009
  613.9071'073--dc22
                                                               2009030455

Published by Nova Science Publishers, Inc. ✢ *New York*

Contents

Preface		xi
Chapter 1	Comprehensive Sex Education Curricula *The Administration for Children and Families (ACF) and Department of Health and Human Services (HHS)*	1
Chapter 2	Teen Pregnancy *Centers for Disease Control and Prevention*	45
Chapter Sources		53
Index		55

PREFACE

Comprehensive Sex Education. The Sex Education curricula for adolescents have been endorsed by various governmental agencies, educational organizations, and teenage advocacy groups as the most effective educational method for reducing teenage pregnancy and helping prevent the spread of sexually transmitted diseases (STDs) among America's youth. This book presents the latest research on this field of study.

Chapter 1 - "Comprehensive Sex Education" curricula for adolescents have been endorsed by various governmental agencies, educational organizations, and teenage advocacy groups as the most effective educational method for reducing teenage pregnancy and helping prevent the spread of sexually transmitted diseases (STDs) among America's youth. The National Institutes of Health (NIH) defines Comprehensive Sex Education (CSE) as "teaching both abstinence and the use of protective methods for sexually active youth"; NIH states that CSE curricula have been "shown to delay sexual activity among teens." Non-governmental groups that support CSE have also made statements linking CSE curricula to abstinence as well as reduction of pregnancy and sexually transmitted infections (STIs).

The Administration for Children and Families, within the Department of Health and Human Services undertook an examination of some of the most common CSE curricula currently in use. The purpose of this examination was to inform federal policymakers of the content, medical accuracy, and effectiveness of CSE curricula currently in use.

Chapter 2 - About one-third of girls in the United States get pregnant before age 20. In 2006, a total of 435,427 infants were born to mothers aged 15–19 years, a birth rate of 41.9 per 1,000 women in this age group. More than 80% of these births were unintended, meaning they occurred sooner than desired or were not wanted at any time. In the United States, rates for pregnancy, birth, sexually transmitted diseases (STDs), and abortion among teenagers are considerably higher than rates in Canada, England, France, Ireland, the Netherlands, Sweden, Japan, and most other developed countries.

In: Sexuality Education
Editor: Kelly N. Stanton

ISBN: 978-1-60692-153-1
© 2010 Nova Science Publishers, Inc.

Chapter 1

COMPREHENSIVE SEX EDUCATION CURRICULA

The Administration for Children and Families (ACF) and Department of Health and Human Services (HHS)

INTRODUCTION

"Comprehensive Sex Education" curricula for adolescents have been endorsed by various governmental agencies, educational organizations, and teenage advocacy groups as the most effective educational method for reducing teenage pregnancy and helping prevent the spread of sexually transmitted diseases (STDs) among America's youth. The National Institutes of Health (NIH) defines Comprehensive Sex Education (CSE) as "teaching both abstinence and the use of protective methods for sexually active youth"; NIH states that CSE curricula have been "shown to delay sexual activity among teens."[1] Non-governmental groups that support CSE have also made statements linking CSE curricula to abstinence as well as reduction of pregnancy and sexually transmitted infections (STIs).[2]

The Administration for Children and Families, within the Department of Health and Human Services undertook an examination of some of the most common CSE curricula currently in use. The purpose of this examination was to inform federal policymakers of the content, medical accuracy, and effectiveness of CSE curricula currently in use.

BACKGROUND

In 2005, Senators Santorum and Coburn requested that the Administration for Children and Families (ACF) review and evaluate comprehensive sex education programs supported with federal dollars. The Senators wrote to the Assistant Secretary for Children and Families,

> "In particular, we would appreciate a review that explores the effectiveness of these programs in reducing teen pregnancy rates and the transmission of sexually transmitted diseases. In addition, please assess the effectiveness of these programs in advancing the greater goal of encouraging teens to make the healthy decision to delay sexual activity. Please also include an evaluation of the scientific accuracy of the content of these programs. Finally, we would appreciate an assessment of how the actual content of these programs compares to their stated goals."

In response, ACF contracted with the Sagamore Institute for Policy Research to review some of the most common CSE curricula currently in use. ACF also requested and received comments on these reviews from the Medical Institute for Sexual Health (MISH).

RESEARCH QUESTIONS AND METHODOLOGY

In response to the request from Senators Santorum and Coburn, the curriculum reviews evaluated four questions:

1. Does the content of the comprehensive sex education curricula mirror the stated purposes?
2. What is the content of comprehensive sex education curricula?
3. Do comprehensive sex education curricula contain medically inaccurate statements?
4. Do evaluations of these curricula show them to be effective at (a) delaying sexual debut and (b) reducing sex without condoms?

The initial charge of this project was to evaluate the content and effectiveness of the "most frequently used" CSE curricula. After a thorough search, which included contacting publishers, researchers, distributors, and advocacy groups, it was determined that a list ranked by "frequency of use" or "number of copies purchased" was not in existence nor could one be produced. Instead, curricula were chosen for this study based on the frequency and strength of endorsement received from leading and recognized sexuality information organizations and resources.[3] A curriculum was considered to be "endorsed" if a source recommended it or promoted it as a "program that works." The curricula mentioned most frequently were chosen for this study if they were school-based (i.e. not solely for community organizations), widely available, and described by at least one source as "comprehensive" or "abstinence-plus." Additional weight was given to curricula described as evidence-based or as a "program that works."

It should be noted that some of the curricula reviewed do not state in their materials that they have an abstinence focus — i.e. that they are "comprehensive sex education," "abstinence plus," or in some other way focused on abstinence. However, if a curriculum were endorsed as "comprehensive" or "abstinence plus" by a leading sexuality information organization and resources, it was assumed that the curriculum would be purchased and used for the purpose of providing comprehensive sex education. Additionally of note, some of the curricula have recently published revisions with added abstinence components. In every case, the most recent version of the curricula available was studied.

Nine curricula met the criteria for this study and were subsequently reviewed:

1. *Reducing the Risk: Building Skills to Prevent Pregnancy, STD & HIV (4*th *Edition)*, by R. Barth, 2004.
2. *Be Proud! Be Responsible!*, L. Jemmott, J. Jemmott, K. McCaffree, published by Select Media, Inc. 2003.
3. *Safer Choices: Preventing HIV, Other STD and Pregnancy (Level 1)*, by J. Fetro, R. Barth, K. Coyle, published by ETR Associates, 1998; and *Safer Choices: Preventing HIV, Other STD and Pregnancy (Level 2)*, by K. Coyle and J. Fetro, published by ETR Associates, 1998.
4. *AIDS Prevention for Adolescents in School,* by S. Kasen, and I. Tropp, distributed by the Program Archive on Sexuality, Health, and Adolescence (PASHA), 2003.
5. *BART=Becoming a Responsible Teen (Revised Edition),* by J. Lawrence, published by ETR (Education, Training, Research) Associates, 2005.

6. *Teen Talk: An Adolescent Pregnancy Prevention Program,* by M. Eisen, A. McAlister, G. Zellman, distributed by PASHA, 2003.
7. *Reach for Health, Curriculum*[4], *Grade 8,* by L. O'Donnell, et al., by Education Development Center, Inc., 2003.
8. *Making Proud Choices.* L. Jemmott, J. Jemmott, K. McCaffree, published by Select Media, Inc., 2001, 2002.
9. *Positive Images: Teaching Abstinence, Contraception, and Sexual Healthy,* by P. Brick and B. Taverner, published by Planned Parenthood of Greater Northern New Jersey, Inc., 2001.

The curriculum review consisted of four components. First, each curriculum underwent an extensive content analysis, i.e. a word-by-word count of instances in which certain words or themes (e.g. condoms, abstinence) are mentioned. Content analyses offer insight into the weight respective curricula give to key themes. Appendix A contains the complete content analysis for each curriculum reviewed.

Second, the stated purposes of the curricula were compared to the actual emphases of the curricula, as demonstrated by the content analysis.

Third, curriculum content was evaluated for medical accuracy, primarily the accuracy of statements about condoms (including statements on a common spermicide, nonoxynol-9, that was previously recommended to be added to condoms).

Lastly, evaluations of each curriculum — which offer insights into curriculum effectiveness at delaying sexual debut and increasing condom use — were located and summarized.

Appendix B contains a curriculum-by-curriculum review of the each curriculum's content, medical accuracy, and evaluations of each curriculum.

FINDINGS

The curriculum reviews yielded the following findings:

- **Does the content of the curricula mirror their stated purposes?**
  While the content of the curricula reviewed adheres to their stated purposes for the most part, these curricula often do not spend as much time discussing abstinence as they do discussing contraception and ways to lessen risks of sexual activity. Of the curricula reviewed, the curriculum with the most balanced discussion of abstinence and safer-

sex still discussed condoms and contraception nearly seven times more than abstinence.[5] Three of the nine curricula reviewed did not have a stated purpose of promoting abstinence; however, two of these three curricula still discussed abstinence as an option (although, again, discussion of condoms and safer sex predominated). As a last note, it is important to recognize that, although some of the curricula do not include abstinence as a stated purpose, some sexuality information organizations and resources recommend these curricula as comprehensive sex education.

- **What is the content of comprehensive sex education curricula?** As mentioned in the previous paragraph, these curricula focus on contraception and ways to lessen risks of sexual activity, although abstinence is at times a non-trivial component. Curriculum approaches to discussing contraception and ways to lessen risks of sexual activity can be grouped in three broad areas: (1) how to obtain protective devices (e.g. condoms), (2) how to broach a discussion on introducing these devices in a relationship, and (3) how to correctly use the devices. Below are a few excerpts from the curricula in these three areas.

    - **How to obtain protective devices:** "How can you minimize your embarrassment when buying condoms? ... Take a friend along; find stores where you don't have to ask for condoms (e.g. stocked on open counter or shelf); wear shades or a disguise so no one will recognize you; have a friend or sibling who isn't embarrassed buy them for you; make up a condom request card that you can hand to the store clerk (Show example)" *(AIDS Prevention for Adolescents in School,* p. 63).

    - **How to broach a discussion on introducing these devices in a relationship:** "Teacher states: "Pretend I am your sexual partner. I am going to read more excuses (for not using condoms) and I want you to convince me to use a condom" *(Making Proud Choices,* p. 157).

    - **How to correctly use the devices:** "Have volunteers come to the front of the room (preferably an equal number of males and females). Distribute one card to each. Give them a few minutes to arrange themselves in the proper order so their cards illustrate effective condom use from start to finish. Non-participants observe how the group completes this task and review the final order. When the order is correct, post the cards in the front of the room. CORRECT ORDER: (Sexual Arousal, Erection, Leave Room at the Tip, Roll Condom On, Intercourse, Orgasm/Ejaculation, Hold Onto Rim, Withdraw the Penis, Loss of Erection, Relaxation). Ask a volunteer to describe each step in condom use, using the index and middle finger or a model of a penis" *(Positive Images,* p. 102).

- **Do the curricula contain medically inaccurate statements?** Most comprehensive sex education curricula reviewed contain some level of medical inaccuracy. Of the nine curricula reviewed, three had no medically inaccurate statements.[6] The most common type of medical inaccuracy involved promotion of nonoxynol-9, a common spermicide; three curricula had medical inaccuracies involving nonoxynol-9.[7] While condoms with nonoxynol-9 (N-9) had previously been recommended for reducing the risk of HIV and other STD in the 1990s, research over the last decade has demonstrated that nonxynol-9 is at best ineffective against STDs and HIV, and at worse increases risk.[8]

Other inaccuracies included: (a) one curriculum that used the term "dental dam" instead of the FDA-approved "rubber dam"[9]; (b) one curriculum that quoted first year condom failure rates for pregnancy at 12%, when the correct statistic is 15%[10]; and (c) one curriculum that stated that all condoms marketed in the United States "meet federal assurance standards" (which is not true).[11]

In terms of inaccurate statistics related to condom effectiveness, eight of the nine curricula did not have any inaccuracies. The one curriculum which did have inaccuracies, *Making Proud Choices,* had three erroneous statements.[12]

Although there were few inaccurate statements regarding condom effectiveness, the curricula do not state the risks of condom failure as extensively as is done in some abstinence-until-marriage curricula, nor do they discuss condom failure rates in context. Indeed, there were misleading statements in every curriculum reviewed. For example, one curriculum states, "When used correctly, latex condoms prevent pregnancy 97% of the time."[13] While this statement is technically true,[14] 15% percent of women using condoms for contraception experience an unintended pregnancy during the first year of "typical use,"[15] and 20% of adolescents under the age of 18 using condoms for contraception get pregnant within one year.[16]

For perspective, it may be helpful to compare the error rate reported here with statistics cited in the December 2004 report entitled "The Content of Federally Funded Abstinence Education Programs," which is typically called the Waxman Report.[17] This report found that, of thirteen abstinence-until-marriage curricula reviewed, eleven contained medically inaccurate statements; in all thirteen curricula (nearly 5,000 pages of information), there were 49 instances of questionable information.[18] It could easily be argued that the comprehensive sex education curricula reviewed for this report have a similar rate of error compared with abstinence-until-marriage curricula.

- **Do evaluations of these curricula show them to be effective at (a) delaying sexual debut and (b) reducing sex without condoms?**
  According to the evaluations reviewed, these curricula show some small positive impacts on (b) reducing sex without condoms, and to a lesser extent (a) delaying sexual debut. Specifically, there were evaluations for eight of the nine curricula reviewed. Of those eight curricula, seven showed at least some positive impacts on condom use; two showed some positive impacts on delay of sexual initiation.[19] One curriculum *(Teen Talk)* showed the only negative impact: for sexually inexperienced females, there was a negative impact on first intercourse and on consistent use of contraceptives. Often the impacts observed in evaluations are small, and most often the impacts do not extend three or six months after a curriculum has been used.[20] It is important to note that evaluations of the curricula do have limitations. All curricula were evaluated by the curriculum authors themselves (although all evaluations were peer- reviewed and published in established journals). Also, the sample sizes are small in some of the evaluations, and research design issues decrease the ability to draw conclusions from some of the evaluations. Appendix B contains details on the evaluations of these curricula.

CONCLUSION

Research on the effectiveness of nine commonly used comprehensive sex education curricula demonstrates that, while such curricula show small positive impacts on increasing condom use among youth, only a couple of curricula show impacts on delaying sexual debut; moreover, effects most often disappear over time. The fact that both the stated purposes and the actual content of these curricula emphasize ways to lessen risks associated with sexual activity — and not necessarily avoiding sexual activity — may explain why research shows them to be more effective at increasing condom use than at delaying sexual debut. Lastly, although the medical accuracy of comprehensive sex education curricula is nearly 100% — similar to that of abstinence-until-marriage curricula — efforts could be made to more extensively detail condom failure rates in context.

APPENDIX A: CONTENT ANALYSIS

Provided below is a word-by-word count of the number of times specific words or themes appears in each of the reviewed curricula.

	RTR	Be Proud	SC 1	SC 2	AIDS	BART	Teen Talk	Reach	MPC	PI
100% safe/effective	4	22	7	1	4	0	5	12	1	7
abortion/termination/interruption	1	0	0	1	0	0	8	0	0	18
abstinence/abstain	90	50	5	5	0	19	32	15	18	87
alcohol	3	14	2	3	5	12	2	0	18	21
alternatives to sexual intercourse	45	10	64	40	1	7	0	5	12	16
anal sex	11	33	10	2	4	16	0	1	57	8
avoid/avoiding (behaviors/consequences)	20	9	24	1	0	14	11	9	42	18
birth control	27	5	25	25	9	5	58	10	37	37
boyfriend (s)	24	13	1	3	11	8	2	11	23	7
casual sex	0	0	0	0	0	0	0	0	0	0
cervical cap	0	0	1	0	0	0	8	0	5	15
chlamydia	5	0	16	7	1	0	5	2	6	1
committed relationship	0	2	0	0	0	1	0	1	0	1
condom/contraceptive failure	1	3	5	5	0	0	0	0	2	7

Appendix A. (Continued)

	RTR	Be Proud	SC 1	SC 2	AIDS	BART	Teen Talk	Reach	MPC	PI
condom/condoms	183	495	383	389	136	262	22	8	650	235
contraception/contraceptive	18	3	31	38	2	0	131	3	39	381
diaphragm	0	0	3	2	0	0	31	0	7	26
douche/douching	8	0	11	10	0	0	14	5	10	2
Drug/drugs	32	58	20	8	36	45	2	2	81	75
ejaculate (tion, s, ed, "cum")	6	14	10	11	0	5	9	18	24	12
emotional (consequences)	2	0	0	0	0	0	1	2	1	0
erection (erect)	1	12	9	9	3	0	8	7	15	19
fantasy (ies, ize)	0	3	0	0	0	0	2	9	5	0
French kissing	2	1	1	0	0	0	0	0	1	1
fun (of sex)	0	24	0	1	0	0	0	0	19	0
genital warts/warts	1	0	8	4	0	0	6	1	11	1
girlfriend	31	13	3	3	6	8	3	6	24	3
gonorrhea	5	1	16	7	2	0	12	3	20	2
health/healthy	27	39	58	60	16	72	77	54	35	180
healthier/healthiest	2	2	0	0	0	1	0	1	3	1
Herpes	4	1	15	6	0	0	20	5	18	1
HIV/AIDS	451	477	369	253	28	473	20	7	210	48
IUD	0	0	4	6	0	0	0	0	0	5
kiss, kissing, kissed, kisses	29	30	15	14	2	8	0	4	33	6
love, loved, loves	51	9	35	19	6	16	0	14	22	14
lovers	1	1	0	0	0	0	0	0	1	1
making love (love making)	0	0	1	1	0	0	0	0	1	1
marriage	3	0	4	1	0	0	1	0	0	9
marry, married	3	0	0	5	1	0	4	0	0	4
masturbation, masturbate	4	5	0	0	0	3	8	2	9	13
masturbation: mutual/partner	1	2	0	0	0	0	1	0	3	0
maximum protection	0	1	0	0	0	0	0	0	0	0
morning after pill (emergency contraception)	0	0	6	12	0	0	1	0	0	24
negative, negatively, (ism)	2	18	12	27	6	10	4	22	14	18
negotiation (to use condoms)	1	37	4	1	14	35	1	0	52	1
no risk	0	0	0	0	2	0	0	3	1	
not having sex	8	0	7	7	7	1	2	3	0	0
oral sex	10	36	9	2	3	13	0	2	73	4
orgasm	1	15	0	0	0	0	6	1	8	11
outercourse	0	2	0	0	0	0	0	0	0	13
parents/parenthood	104	0	97	118	5	34	11	13	13	65
pill (contraceptive)	45	13	37	35	7	4	27	3	31	59
pleasure, able, ing (re: sex)	0	31	2	1	1	0	3	3	8	8

Appendix A. (Continued)

	RTR	Be Proud	SC 1	SC 2	AIDS	BART	Teen Talk	Reach	MPC	PI
practice (s, ed, ing) (techniques, skills, using condoms)	2	5	13	14	0	6	19	47	70	20
pregnant, pregnancy	348	30	167	242	3	8	155	113	184	241
prophylactics	1	0	1	1	0	0	2	0	0	0
protect (s, ed), protection	254	25	314	145	7	24	7	20	82	80
protective (products)	1	10	6	0	0	0	0	0	0	1
purchasing (buying) condoms	2	6	11	12	8	10	4	0	12	5
rape	0	1	0	0	0	0	0	0	2	3
rape: date	0	0	0	0	0	0	0	0	2	1
refuse, refusal (skills)/delaying sex tactics	110	11	84	76	1	13	2	48	46	0
reproductive, reproduction	0	0	5	4	0	0	33	18	2	80
risk reduction	0	0	0	1	0	2	0	0	3	0
risk (high)	4	4	0	0	4	5	4	0	5	3
risk (low, lower)	1	0	0	0	0	1	1	0	1	2
risk, risks, risking	273	166	133	112	32	149	31	38	118	140
riskier	0	0	0	0	0	2	0	0	0	0
risky	8	25	9	5	21	42	2	2	18	2
rubber (s)	8	3	2	2	0	5	24	0	4	4
safe, safely	11	41	8	7	3	67	8	4	40	12
safer	0	74	297	345	2	55	0	0	61	38
safest	6	1	45	26	2	0	1	0	1	0
sex	290	334	442	287	64	168	91	168	440	83
sexual	71	152	106	81	101	94	78	116	146	232
intercourse (sexual)	46	47	81	46	77	23	22	28	58	237
sexual orientation (gay, lesbian, homosexual, same sex)	5	19	7	2	0	6	1	2	9	13
sexuality	18	0	17	19	1	3	32	115	1	98
sexually	47	46	18	23	11	33	38	49	60	85
sexy	2	1	0	1	1	0	0	4	2	0
spermicide (s, dal)	14	11	35	19	4	15	25	4	43	23
sponge	0	0	0	0	0	0	4	0	0	28
STD (s)	230	44	221	178	2	8	47	77	281	2
STI	0	0	0	0	0	0	0	0	0	64
syphilis	0	2	15	4	2	0	12	0	17	1
unprotected sex/intercourse	54	26	43	0	0	23	13	8	30	5
contraceptive film	3	0	6	5	0	0	0	0	6	4

Appendix A. (Continued)

	RTR	Be Proud	SC 1	SC 2	AIDS	BART	Teen Talk	Reach	MPC	PI
venereal disease (VD)	0	0	0	0	0	0	3	0	0	0
withdrawal (withdraws, pull out)	10	3	12	0	0	6	9	4	13	17

RTR = Reducing the Risk
Be Proud = Be Proud, Be Responsible
SC1 = Safer Choices 1
SC2 = Safer Choices 2
AIDS = AIDS Prevention for Adolescents in School
BART = Becoming A Responsible Teen
Teen Talk
Reach = Reach for Health
MPC = Making Proud Choices
PI = Positive Images

APPENDIX B: CURRICULUM-BY-CURRICULUM REVIEW

Provided below is a curriculum-by-curriculum review of each curriculum's content (as compared to its stated purposes) and medical accuracy, as well as the findings from evaluations of each curriculum.

Curriculum 1: Reducing the Risk: Building Skills to Prevent Pregnancy, STD & HIV

"Reducing the Risk: Building Skills to Prevent Pregnancy, STD & HIV" Curriculum Description

Program Author: R. Barth, 2004.

- *In collaboration with:* ETR Associates, a creator/publisher of health education materials; original edition published in 1989; the current edition was published by ETR in 2004.
- *Funded by:* Grants from the Stuart Foundation and the Centers for Disease Control and Prevention.

- Distributed by: ETR Associates.

Format: A sixteen class format.

- *Audience:* Targeted for high school students, particularly 9th and 10th graders.

Stated Goals/Focus: The objectives of this 16-lesson curriculum are to help students:

- evaluate the risks and consequences of teen pregnancy and STD infection (including HIV);
- understand factual information and recognize that abstinence and contraception are the only ways to avoid pregnancy, HIV and other STDs;
- build effective communication skills for remaining abstinent and avoiding unprotected sexual intercourse.

"Reducing the Risk: Building Skills to Prevent Pregnancy, STD & HIV" Curriculum Content

Reducing the Risk emphasizes ways to lessen risks of sexual activity ("protection" is mentioned 254 times, and "condoms" are mentioned 183 times), although there is a larger mention of abstinence (90) in this curriculum than in any other curriculum reviewed for this study *(Positive Images* mentions abstinence the second-highest number of times, at 87 mentions). The curriculum also makes some effort to differentiate abstinence from other sexual activity: there are 4 references to "100%," 6 references to "safest" in connection to abstinence being the safest choice, and 8 references to "not having sex." Marriage (or a form of the word) is mentioned 6 times. Appendix A lists the content analysis for this and all other curricula reviewed.

Examples of curriculum content :

- "For teenagers, abstinence from sex and needle use are the best choices. The second best choice is to use condoms. The third best choice is to avoid having multiple partners" (p. 29).
- (In section on Implementing Protection from STD and Pregnancy:)

    - STEP 2: Preparing for Protection
    - 2. Get the condoms and foam.

- Who will get them? When? Where? What problems might arise in getting them? "What would you do then?
- STEP 3: Using Protection
- 3. Use the condoms and foam.
- Whose job would it be to carry the protection? Who would bring out the condoms and foam? What would he/she say? What would be the most romantic way to use the condom and foam? What might go wrong? What would you do to save the evening?" (p. 190).

- "At some time in their lives, most people decide they are ready to have sex but not to become a parent. To have sex but not become a parent or become infected with an STD, people must consistently and effectively use protection" (p. 97).
- (Truth or Myth) "Teenagers can obtain birth control pills from family planning clinics and doctors without permission from a parent. TRUTH. You do not need a parent's permission to get birth control at a clinic. No one needs to know that you are going to a clinic" (p. 137).
- (On a "Shopping Information Homework" assignment) "Tell students to fill in all information for 3 kinds of condoms and 1 type of foam. The brand name is the maker of the product. For condoms, also indicate whether the product is lubricated and has a reservoir or plain tip. After students leave the store, they should complete items 3 and 4 to indicate how comfortable they were there and whether they would recommend the store to a friend. Put down the store's hours, too, because it may be important to know where to get protection at some odd hours" (p. 113).

"Reducing the Risk: Building Skills to Prevent Pregnancy, STD & HIV"
Medical Accuracy

There were no medically inaccurate statements in the curriculum; however, there were three statements that did not provide explicit details of condom failure rates. For example:

- "Condoms made of latex provide good protection from HIV when used correctly and consistently during vaginal, anal or oral sex" (p. 110.)

- "If a condom is used correctly together with foam (see below) every time a couple has sex, the combined method will work almost all of the time to prevent pregnancy" (p. 104).
- "Condoms are most effective preventing diseases that are spread through contact with semen, vaginal secretion or blood. Reliable scientific studies prove they are very effective in preventing HIV. The best studies to date indicate they also reduce the risk for gonorrhea, Chlamydia and trichomoniasis, although further studies are being done in this area" (p. 204).

"Good," "almost all the time," and "very effective" are all subjective terms. It should also be noted that, contrary to the claim in the last quote, the 2001 NIH report on condom effectiveness found insufficient evidence to suggest that condoms reduce trichomoniasis risk.[21]

"Reducing the Risk: Building Skills to Prevent Pregnancy, STD & HIV"
Evaluations of Curriculum Effectiveness
Kirby and Barth, 1991.[22]

- Background and methodology: conducted by curriculum's author; published in Family Planning Perspectives; sample size of 758; mixed grades and ethnicities.
- Findings:

  - No impact on frequency of intercourse.
  - No impact on initiation of first sex at 6 months.
  - Statistically significant, positive impact on initiation of first sex at 18 months (significantly fewer virgins had become active in the study group than in the control group).
  - No impact on contraceptive use at first intercourse.
  - No overall increased use of contraceptives at 18 month follow-up (small impact on subgroups but some subgroups had small sample sizes, making causality suspect).
  - No overall impact on unprotected sex at 18 months.
  - No impact on pregnancy rates.

Hubbard, Giese, and Rainey, 1998.[23]

- Background and methodology: published in Journal of School Health; sample size of 212; attrition rate of 58%.
- Findings:
  - Increased condom use among those who were sexually inexperienced at pre-test.
  - Delayed initiation of first sex.

Curriculum 2: Be Proud! Be Responsible!

This program is part of a three-curricula collection, including *Making Proud Choices* and *Making a Difference*. *Making Proud Choices* is reviewed later in this appendix; *Making a Difference,* an abstinence-based intervention, was not reviewed. All curricula are by the same authors.

"Be Proud! Be Responsible!" Curriculum Description
Program Authors: L. Jemmott, J. Jemmott III, K. McCaffree, 2003.

- *Funded by:* The American Foundation for AIDS Research (AMFAR). The National Institute for Child Health and Human Development (NICHD) provided funding for an evaluation of this material with inner-city junior high school students, and it was adapted for use with both in-school and out-of-school youth with funds from AMFAR and the State of New Jersey Department of Health.
- *Distributed by:* Select Media of New York

Format: Six 50-minute sessions, presented over 1-5 days, or in a classroom setting over a number of weeks.

- *Audience:* Targets youth between the ages of 13 and 19.

Stated Goals/Focus: The stated goals are:

- to reduce unprotected sex among sexually active inner-city youth;
- to delay initiation of sex among sexually inexperienced youth; and
- to help youth make proud and responsible sexual decisions. This curriculum focuses almost exclusively on HIV/AIDS risk reduction,

with only a couple of brief mentions of pregnancy prevention and other STDs.

"Be Proud! Be Responsible!" Curriculum Content

This curriculum has a slightly higher emphasis on abstaining from sex than other curricula reviewed; however, a far greater prominence is placed on condom use and "safer sex," and lowering "risks." For example, there are 77 references to "abstinence" or things that are "100% safe/effective," while there are 495 references to condoms. Appendix A lists the content analysis for this and all other curricula reviewed.

Examples of curriculum content:

- "Once you and a partner agree to use condoms, do something positive and fun. Go to the store together. Buy lots of different brands and colors. Plan a special day when you can experiment. Just talking about how you'll use all of those condoms can be a turn on" (p. 82).
- "Showering together" is a "green light" (no risk) activity (p. 60).
- Learning objective: "Identify ways to make condoms a more pleasurable part of the sexual experience" (p. 73).
- In order for a curriculum to effectively reduce adolescent risk of HIV infection, it must dispel beliefs that condoms interfere with sexual pleasure" (p. 8).
- "Additional Ideas ... Use condoms as a method of foreplay...Use different colors and types/textures (some have ribs on them)... Think up a sexual fantasy using condoms... Tell your partner how using a condom can make a man last longer... Act sexy/sensual when putting condoms on... Have a sense of humor—be silly—make jokes...Hide them on your body and ask your partner to find it...Wrap them as a present and give them to your partner before a romantic dinner... Tease each other manually while putting on the condom... Have fun putting them on your partner— pretend you are different people or in different situations" (p. 81).
- "Q: If a man lost his erection after putting on a condom and before intercourse, what could the couple do? A: Continue stimulating one another, relax and enjoy the fun, wait a while and start playing again using the condom as part of the play. Emphasize that this will probably happen to most males at some point in their lives" (p. 82).
- "Q: Most people don't know that condoms can be a pleasant part of the experience with each other because using them is so new. How

can people make condoms feel good and be fun? A: Have your partner play with you and/or roll a condom on, put lubricant and spermicide inside to make them feel wet, use colored or decorated condoms, etc" (p. 82).
- "Excuse (for not using a condom): When I stop to put it on, I'll lose my erection. (Instructed) Response: Don't worry, I'll help you get it back" (p. 92).
- "Excuse (for not using a condom): But we've been having sex without condoms for a while. (Instructed) Response: I know, but we could enjoy each other a lot more if I did not have to worry. And I wouldn't worry if we used condoms" (p. 93).
- "Many young women do not reach orgasm during vaginal intercourse, especially when they and their partners are just learning about sex. Most women need to have their clitoris (the arousal organ in their vulvas) touched, or indirectly in order to have an orgasm. This sometimes happens during intercourse, but only if a partner rubs it manually or with the pelvis" (p. 128).
- "Although some guys may be uncomfortable with a young woman who is very assertive, most guys get very turned on if their partner touches them, especially if she touches his penis and strokes it. Applying lubrication directly on his penis will probably make him very excited. Then she can roll the condom on with a lot of lubrication inside and out. During this entire time, her own arousal level also will increase, preparing her vagina for a comfortable penetration" (p. 128).
- "Using a condom also can make a male's erection last longer. Most men say that the longer they are stimulated without having an orgasm, the better the orgasm feels when they have it. This means he won't have an orgasm before he wants to and that may help his partner enjoy sex more. Since many women need more stimulation to have an orgasm, having him stay hard longer is beneficial" (p. 128).

"Be Proud! Be Responsible!" Medical Accuracy

There were two medically inaccurate statements in this curriculum, both involving the spermicide nonoxynol-9:

- "What can a person use in addition to a condom that might provide additional protection against HIV? Nonoxynol-9 or spermicide" (p. 161).

- "When they are used in conjunction with a spermicide such as Nonoxynol-9, condoms become even more effective in preventing disease transmission" (p. 173).

While condoms with the spermicide nonoxynol-9 (N-9) had previously been recommended for reducing the risk of HIV and other STD, this is a serious medical error.

The curriculum does not provide elaborate details on condom failure; for example, the curriculum states,

- "Studies of couples using condoms to prevent pregnancy produce failure rate from less than 1 percent to 22 percent. Although proper use greatly reduces the risk of condom failure, condoms are not 100 percent effective" (p. 143).

The curriculum also uses inaccurate language; for example, the curriculum states,

- "When performing oral sex on a woman, you can protect yourself and your partner by placing a dental dam over the vulva (the entire outer region of the vagina, including the clitoris and the vaginal opening). You can make your own dental dam by slitting a condom the long way and opening it up" (page not referenced).

Although "rubber dams" have been approved by the FDA, nothing under the term "dental dam" has been approved by the FDA.

"Be Proud! Be Responsible!" Evaluations of Curriculum Effectiveness
Jemmott, Jemmott, & Fong, 1992.[24]

- Background and methodology: Conducted by the curriculum's authors; published in the American Journal of Public Health; sample size 157 students, all African- American males; no long-term follow-up — only 3-month post-test.
- Findings:
  - No impact on whether participants engaged in sexual behavior.
  - Lowered number of sexual partners at 3 months.
  - Increased frequency of condom use at 3 months.

Jemmott, Jemmott, Fong, & McCaffree, 1999[25]

- Background and methodology: Conducted by curriculum's authors; published in the American Journal of Community Psychology; replicated 1992 study with larger sample size (496) of African-American males and females; included both a 3 and 6 month follow-up; relatively small attrition rate (3.2% at 3 months, 7.3% at 6 months).
- Findings:

  - Unlike the previous study, this evaluation found no significant differences at the 3 month follow-up in sexual behaviors deemed as "risky."
  - At 6 month follow-up, there was no significant difference between the control and study groups regarding their beliefs that condoms can prevent pregnancy and STDs.
  - Experimental group scored higher on AIDS knowledge than the control group.
  - Respondents of the experimental group reported great self-efficacy regarding condom use, but the effects were small.

Curriculum 3: Safer Choices 1 & 2: A High School Based Program to Prevent STDs, HIV & Pregnancy

"Safer Choices 1 & 2: A High School Based Program to Prevent STDs, HIV & Pregnancy" Curriculum Description
Program Authors: K. Coyle and J. Fetro, 1998

- *In collaboration with:* the Center for Health Promotion R&D at the University of Texas-Houston.
- *Funded by:* A contract with the Centers for Disease Control and Prevention, Division of Adolescent School Health.
- *Distributed by:* ETR Associates

Format: Level 1 (for 9th graders) and Level 2 (for 10th graders) are each 10-lesson units, with each lesson designed for a 45-minute class period.

- *Audience:* High school, specifically 9th and 10th grade students.

Stated Goals/Focus: The curriculum's stated purpose is to prevent HIV infection, other STDs and unintended pregnancy in high school students by reducing the number of students who have sexual intercourse and by encouraging condom use among those who do have sex. The material includes information on HIV and five other sexually transmitted diseases.

"Safer Choices 1 & 2: A High School Based Program to Prevent STDs, HIV & Pregnancy" Curriculum Content

This curriculum emphasizes contraception, with 383 mentions of condoms in Safer Choices 1 and 389 in Safer Choices 2. There are only five mentions of the word "abstinence" in each curriculum, although there are 45 references to the word "safest" and 7 to "not having sex" in Safer Choices 1 (26 and 7, respectively, in Safer Choices 2). Of all curricula reviewed, *Safer Choices 1* had the highest mention of "alternatives" (64), that is, discussing skills to get out of a situation where a student is feeling pressured to have sex. Appendix A lists the content analysis for this and all other curricula reviewed.

Examples of curriculum content:

- "Condoms can be fun" (Level 2, p. 207).
- (Homework assignment) "Tell students that they will do a homework assignment in pairs. Explain that, with their partners, they should go to a local market or drugstore to gather information about protective products, such as condoms and vaginal spermicides. After finding the protective products they should complete the homework, identifying what types of protection are available, how much they cost, and whether they are accessible to teens who may want to purchase them. Finally, they should decide how comfortable they would be buying protection in that store and whether they would recommend that store to a friend, and explain why or why not" (Level 1, p. 191).
- "Studies of hundreds of couples show that consistent condom use is possible when people have the skills and motivation to do so. One of the biggest motivations in deciding to use any product—whether it's detergent or a condom—is the belief the product will work. Scientific studies have clearly demonstrated that condoms are highly effective in preventing HIV and other STD transmission. The majority of Americans know condoms work when they're used as intended. Almost 75 percent of people older than 18 believe condoms are effective in preventing HIV infection. People who believe a product

will work are more likely to use it. That's why it's so important to correct misinformation about condoms. People who are skeptical about condoms aren't as likely to use them—but that doesn't mean they won't have sex. And unprotected sex puts them at risk for infections with HIV and other STDs. In addition to believing the product will work (product efficacy), people have to believe they will be able to use the product correctly (self-efficacy). That's why it's important to teach people skills in using condoms, such as how to put them on the right way, as well as how to talk with sexual partners about condom use or to say no to sex if a partner refuses to use a condom" (Level 2, pp. 260-261).

"Safer Choices 1 & 2: A High School Based Program to Prevent STDs, HIV & Pregnancy" Medical Accuracy

There is one inaccurate statement in this curriculum:

- In terms of pregnancy prevention, first year failure rates among typical users average about 12%" (p. 247).

The authors missed the mark by 3 percentage points: 15% percent of women using condoms for contraception experience an unintended pregnancy during the first year of "typical use,"[26] and 20% of adolescents under the age of 18 using condoms for contraception get pregnant within one year.[27]

There are 2 misleading statements; for example:

- "When used correctly, latex condoms prevent pregnancy 97% of the time" (Implementation guide, p. 176).
- "Latex condoms can be 98% effective in preventing HIV, STD and pregnancy if used correctly and consistently" (Level 1, Appendix B, page 247; Level 2, Appendix B, p. 233).

While both statements are technically true,[28,29] 15% percent of women using condoms for contraception experience an unintended pregnancy during the first year of "typical use,"[30] and 20% of adolescents under the age of 18 using condoms for contraception get pregnant within one year.[31]

There is another misleading statement:

- "You and your partner did not experience a pregnancy because you used a latex condom and foam every time you had sex" (Level 2, p. 91).

While it is possible that a couple did not become pregnant due to using a condom and contraceptive foam, this is not 100% guaranteed.

"Safer Choices 1 & 2: A High School Based Program to Prevent STDs, HIV & Pregnancy" Evaluation of Curriculum Effectiveness
Coyle, 2001.[32]

- Background and methodology: conducted by curriculum's author; published in Public Health Reports; two-year implementation phase of the research study involved intervention schools; students received their most intensive exposure from the 20- lesson curriculum and school-wide, peer-sponsored events
- Findings[33]:
    - No impact on delaying the initiation of intercourse.
    - No impact on the frequency of sex.
    - No impact on the number of sex partners.
    - Increased use of condoms at "last sex."
    - Decreased the frequency of sex without condoms.
    - Decreased the number of sexual partners without using a condom.

- Other findings[34]:
    - Thirty-one months following the baseline survey, *Safer Choices* reduced the frequency of intercourse without a condom (during the three months prior to the survey), reduced the number of sexual partners with whom students had intercourse without a condom (during the three months prior to the survey), and increased use of condoms and other protection against pregnancy at last intercourse.
    - Thirty-one months following the baseline survey, *Safer Choices'* students, relative to comparison students, scored significantly higher on the HIV and other STD knowledge scales, expressed significantly more positive attitudes about condoms; and reported significantly greater condom use self-efficacy, fewer barriers to

condom use, and higher levels of perceived risk for HIV and other STD. *Safer Choices'* students also reported greater normative beliefs about condom use and communication with parents; these differences neared statistical significance (P=0.06 for each variable).[35]

Curriculum 4: AIDS Prevention for Adolescents in School

"AIDS Prevention for Adolescents in School" Curriculum Description
Program Authors: S. Kasen, I. Tropp, H. Walter, R. Vaughan, et al., 2003.

- *In collaboration with:* The HIV Center for Clinical and Behavioral Studies, The New York State Psychiatric Institute and Columbia University.
- *Funded by:* the National Institute of Mental Health.
- *Distributed by:* the Program Archive on Sexuality, Health and Adolescence (PASHA)[36]

Format: a six-lesson curriculum; one hour per lesson; delivered on six consecutive days

- *Audience:* recommended by PASHA for students in high school or approximately ages 14-19.

Stated Goals/Focus: Goals of this HIV/AIDS prevention curriculum include:

- to increase knowledge about AIDS (cause, prognosis, transmission, prevention, community resources);
- to identify HIV risk factors; and
- to understand the impact of personal values and outside influences on decisions regarding sexual intercourse.

The course seeks to empower students to negotiate delayed involvement in sexual intercourse, to negotiate condom use, and to use condoms effectively.

"AIDS Prevention for Adolescents in School" Curriculum Content
As is evident in the stated goals of the program, the curriculum focuses largely on the acquisition and use of contraceptives. This program makes no

reference to abstinence, committed relationships, or marriage. There were 13 references to a form of "personal values"; these references included conversation on delaying "involvement in sexual intercourse," but there were no discussions on the benefits of abstinence. There is limited discussion of pregnancy prevention; its focus is HIV transmission prevention. Appendix A lists the content analysis for this and all other curricula reviewed.

Examples of curriculum content:

- How can you minimize your embarrassment when buying condoms?... Take a friend along; find stores where you don't have to ask for condoms (e.g. stocked on open counter or shelf); wear "shades or a disguise so no one will recognize you; have a friend or sibling who isn't embarrassed buy them for you; make up a condom request card that you can hand to the store clerk (Show example)." (p. 63)
- From "Vignette #3" entitled, "Sandra and Michael." "Michael had sex without using a condom with Sandra. This happened after Sandra had sex without using a condom with Eddie, who used IV drugs and shared needles. Because of Sandra's experience with Eddie, Michael is at high risk for contracting the AIDS virus. Maria is having sex with Michael and using condoms consistently. Her partner, Michael, is at high risk due to his experience with Sandra. Maria does not know about Michael and Sandra. If she did not insist on using condoms consistently, she would be "very likely' to get infected with the AIDS virus. However, since Maria insists that Michael use a condom, she is only "somewhat likely" to get the AIDS virus. Keep in mind that even though condoms are effective for reducing the risk of infection, they are not 100% effective because they can break or leak." (p. 30.)

"AIDS Prevention for Adolescents in School" Medical Accuracy

There was one medically inaccurate statement in this curriculum:

- "In addition, it is recommended that you use a spermicide containing nonoxynol-9." (p. 19).

While condoms with the spermicide nonoxynol-9 (N-9) had previously been recommended for reducing the risk of HIV and other STD, this is a serious medical error.

Also, the curriculum did not provide elaborate details on condom failure; for example, the curriculum states,

- "If you decide to become sexually active, you should use a condom correctly every time you have sexual intercourse. Latex condoms are the most effective in preventing virus transmission. But, be aware that condoms can break or leak and therefore are not 100% effective."

The curriculum does not detail the different failure rates of condoms, nor the option of abstinence.

"AIDS Prevention for Adolescents in School" Evaluation of Curriculum Effectiveness
Walter & Vaughn, 1993.[37]

- Background and methodology: conducted by two of the curriculum's authors; published in *JAMA, the Journal of the American Medical Association* (1993); 3 month post-test has been evaluated. [38]
- Findings:

    - Had no impact on abstinence or in delaying initiation of sex.
    - Increased consistent condom use.
    - Decreased sexual intercourse with high-risk partners.
    - Increased monogamous relationships.

Curriculum 5: BART = Becoming a Responsible Teen (Revised Edition)

"BART = Becoming a Responsible Teen" Curriculum Description
Program Authors: Janet S. St. Lawrence, 1998, 2005 (rev).

- *In collaboration with:* The Jackson-Hinds Comprehensive Health Center
- *Funded by:* the National Institute of Mental Health. According to the curriculum, *B.A.R. T* is one of a series of research-to-classroom programs funded by the Centers for Disease Control and Prevention's Division of Adolescent School Health.
- *Distributed by:* ETR Associates as an "Evidence-based Program"

Format: an eight-lesson curriculum; sessions are designed for weekly meetings lasting 90-120 minutes.

- *Audience:* 14-18 years old. Targeted to African-American youth, with specific references to HIV/AIDS rates in that population; recommended for after-school programs though still presented in a classroom setting.

Stated Goals/Focus: The stated goals of *B.A.R.T.* include:

- providing essential information about HIV and AIDS;
- teaching ways to handle social and sexual pressures and ways to communicate assertively with friends and potential sexual partners; and
- training in refusal, negotiation and condom use skills.

"BART = Becoming a Responsible Teen" Curriculum Content

This curriculum has 19 references to abstinence; however, as is evident in the stated goals of the program, significantly greater emphasis is placed on condom usage — there are 262 references to condoms. The risks associated with sexual activities other than intercourse are not discussed at length. The curriculum places a high priority on a form of the word "safe." A form of the word "risk" implies that "risky" behavior primarily means not using a condom. Appendix A lists the content analysis for this and all other curricula reviewed.

Examples of curriculum content:

- "(Ask students): Does anyone have a story to share about getting or buying condoms? It can be successful, embarrassing or funny." (p. 158.)
- "Lead the group through a visualization: Close your eyes. Imagine you are walking up to the counter with a box of condoms. You are calm and relaxed. You put down the box of condoms. The clerk rings up your purchase and tells you the price. YOU pay for the condoms and the clerk puts the box in a bag. You say "Thanks" and walk away." (p. 158).
- "Using condoms correctly during sexual activity is a central part of becoming a responsible teen and acting responsibly to protect yourself and others." (P. 164)

- "Daydream safely. Even when you daydream about sex, you can imagine using a latex condom." (p. 244).
- "Keep condoms around at home, in your jacket or purse, and with you. Unless they're nearby when you need them, they won't get used." (p. 144).

"BART = Becoming a Responsible Teen" Medical Accuracy

There were no explicitly medically inaccurate statements. However, the curriculum did not provide elaborate details on condom failure or the benefits of abstinence. For example, the curriculum states,

- "If people don't choose abstinence, they can reduce their risk by always using a latex condom correctly, either alone or with a water-based lubricant, every time they have vaginal, oral or anal sex." (p. 61).

"BART = Becoming a Responsible Teen" Evaluations of Curriculum Effectiveness

St. Lawrence, 1995.[39]

- Background and methodology: conducted by the curriculum's author; original study conducted with African-American adolescents, separated by gender, with fourteen sets of sessions conducted over three years; sample size of 246.
- Findings:
  - Delayed sexual initiation.
  - Decreased number of sex partners.
  - Increased condom use for males having vaginal intercourse.
  - Had no effect on condom use for females having vaginal intercourse.
  - Increased overall condom use for all intercourse.
  - No measures were taken to evaluate pregnancies, births, or STIs.

McGuiness, et al., 2002.[40]

- A second study, published in the Journal of the American Psychiatric Nurses Association, and targeting high-risk female adolescents in foster care found increased knowledge related to condom use and HIV risk.

Curriculum 6: Teen Talk

"Teen Talk" Curriculum Description
Program Authors: M. Eisen, A. McAlister, G. Zellman, 1983-1984; 3rd edition, 2003.

- *In collaboration with:* A team of psychologists at the University of Texas and the RAND Corporation.
- *Funded by:* By the National Institute of Child Health & Human Development, state and private foundation sources.
- *Distributed by:* Copyright by Sociometrics, 2003, and available as part of the Program Archive on Sexuality, Health and Adolescence (PASHA)

Format: A 12-15 hour curriculum.

- *Audience:* Recommended by PASHA for middle school/junior high students, approximately 10-14 years of age. Evaluated with 8th and 9th graders, and field tested with African-American high school freshmen in an urban setting.

Stated Goals/Focus: The authors of the study and the curriculum state the curriculum, "was intended to increase awareness of the probability of personally becoming pregnant or causing a pregnancy; the negative personal consequences of teenage maternity and paternity; and the personal and interpersonal benefits of delayed sexual activity and consistent, effective contraceptive use. It was also designed to decrease the psychological interpersonal and logistical barriers to abstinence or consistent contraceptive use." According to the training manual, *Teen Talk* "focuses on contraception and provides this information in ways that teenagers can understand."[41]

"Teen Talk" Curriculum Content
As is evident by the stated purposes, the emphasis of *Teen Talk* is on ways to lessen risks of sexual activity: there were 155 references to pregnancy and 347 references to contraceptives (although there were only 22 references to

condoms and 24 to rubbers). Abstaining from sexual activity is mentioned 32 times. Appendix A lists the content analysis for this and all other curricula reviewed.

Examples of curriculum content:

- This role play is called "A Trip to the Drugstore." Pairs of teenagers are to pretend they have decided to have sex, and go together to the drugstore to obtain contraception. The group leader plays the clerk at the drugstore. The clerk may or may not ask the embarrassing questions teenagers are afraid of, but you should convey that no matter what goes on in the drugstore, they will be served and will get the contraception they need. You may want to be an agreeable clerk first, then a more difficult one, or difficult, then easier" (Users guide, p. 17).
- "During infancy boys and girls begin to explore their bodies. They often discover that touching the sex organs feels good. They may touch or rub their genitals for pleasure. As they grow older they may learn to stimulate themselves in order to feel pleasant sensations or even come to a climax (have an orgasm). This is called masturbation whether performed by oneself or by a partner" (Users guide, p. 6).
- "Abortion is a fairly simple procedure for ending a pregnancy within the first few months. They usually cost around _____. Abortions are safest if they are done in the first 3 months of pregnancy. They can be performed up through the 5th month, but they are more complicated and more things can go wrong. Anyone who is sexually active and misses their period should get a pregnancy test soon after their period was due. Most clinics that provide contraceptives also do pregnancy tests. It is a simple test done on the woman's urine (or sometimes the blood). One of the tests can give accurate results by the tenth day of conception even before a woman has missed her period. These clinics offer pregnancy counseling to explain the alternatives a woman has when she is faced with an unplanned pregnancy; continuing the pregnancy and keeping the baby or adoption or how and where an abortion is done. The decision is often a difficult one. It is important that any woman who suspects she may be pregnant find out early so she can decide what to do. The results of a pregnancy test, like all information in your medical records, is confidential. The clinic will not tell your parents or anyone else whether you are pregnant (or that you are even coming to the clinic). Abortions are legal and a person,

no matter how young, does not need her parents' permission" (Users guide, p. 19-20).
- "Rubbers are considered a barrier method because they keep the sperm from entering the vagina. They are the most effective barrier method available. The condom is a thin covering placed over the penis to catch the semen from an ejaculation. Show condoms. Have several different brands including lubricated and reservoir tip. Open packages and unroll condoms for students to inspect. You may pass them around. Use plastic model of penis or two fingers for demonstration" (User's guide, p. 6).

"Teen Talk" Medical Accuracy

There are no medically inaccurate statements; however, there are 3 misleading statements in the curriculum. The first misleading statement:

- "Any sexually active person runs the risk of getting an STD, unless certain preventive measures are taken" (Users guide, p. 8).

This statement implies that "certain preventive measures" can eliminate the risks of acquiring an STD, which is not true.

Another misleading statement from the curriculum is:

- "Rubbers are highly effective in reducing the chances of transmitting STDs. Sperm- killing preparations like foam, suppositories, diaphragm jelly or cream, and the sponge help reduce the chances some, because, in addition to killing Sperm, they kill many of the germs that cause STDs" (Users guide, p. 11).

It is unclear how effective "highly effective" actually is. Also, spermicides that contain nonoxynol-9 may increase the risk of acquiring certain STDs.

The last misleading statement is:

- "Abortion is a fairly simple procedure for ending a pregnancy within the first few months" (p. 19).

The curriculum does not quantify "simple." There are, in fact, specific risks associated with an abortion.[42]

"Teen Talk" Evaluations of Curriculum Effectiveness

Eisen, Zellman, and McAllister, 1990.[43]

- Background and methodology: conducted by curriculum's authors; published in Family Planning Perspectives; sample size of 888 13-19 yr-old ethnically diverse youth.'"
- Findings:

  - No impact on overall initiation of intercourse (there was small abstinence effect on males).
  - Regarding contraceptive use for sexually inexperienced youth, for males no impact on contraceptive use at first intercourse, last intercourse, or on consistent use of contraceptives; for females, no impact on last intercourse, negative impact on first intercourse and on consistent use of contraceptives
  - Regarding contraceptive use for sexually experienced youth, for males, no impact on last intercourse; small impact on consistent use of contraceptives; for females, no impact on last intercourse or on consistent use of contraceptives

Curriculum 7: Reach for Health

"Reach for Health" Curriculum Description
Program Author: L. O'Donnell, et al., 1994-1995, revised in 2003.

- *In collaboration with:* The Education Development Center, Inc.
- *Funded by:* The National Institute of Child Health and Human Development and the National Institute for Nursing Research.[45] The module was revised in 2002-2003 with funding from the National Institute of Child Health and Human Development.
- *Distributed by:* the Program Archive on Sexuality, Health and Adolescence (PASHA)[46]

Format: Original curriculum was designed for two year intervention (7th & 8th grade) combined with a community-based service-learning component. Alone, the curriculum is ten lessons for each grade.

- *Audience:* Targeted to urban/minority youth in the 7th and 8th grade.

Stated Goals/Focus: The health curriculum consists of 40 core lessons that focus on three primary health risks faced by urban youth:

- drug and alcohol use;
- violence; and
- sexual behaviors that may result in pregnancy or infection with HIV and other STIs.

"Reach for Health" Curriculum Content

Of the reviewed curricula, *Reach for Health* had the highest representation of words relating the fact that abstaining from sexual activity is the only choice that is 100% effective against pregnancy and STIs. Content related to STIs, HIV, condoms, and negative consequences are all statistically equally addressed. Though a stated goal of this curriculum was addressing alcohol, drug use, and violence related to sexual consequences, there were 0 references to "alcohol," 2 uses of the word "drug/drugs," and 1 reference to "sexual violence." Since the community portion of this program was not addressed, it is assumed that that portion of the program covered those issues. Appendix A lists the content analysis for this and all other curricula reviewed.

Examples of curriculum content:

- [In a section on "understanding sexual attraction" describing various stages of attraction and physical affection:]
  - Get to know the other person better: Have a conversation with the person face to face or on the phone; write a letter to the person; spend time with the person in a group doing activities, such as going to a concert, the mall, or a movie; invite the person to do an activity with you alone.
  - Express your feelings for the person with affectionate touch: hold hands; put your arm around the person; hug; kiss; rub the other person's shoulders; dance together closely.
  - Express your feelings with greater physical intimacy: deep kissing; petting; touching above the waist; touching below the waist; touching without clothes on; touching the other person's sexual organs; having sexual intercourse—vaginal, oral, anal.
  - "Note that these behaviors carry different risks and possible positive or negative consequences. Risk can be defined as anything a person does that increases his or her chances of a harmful outcome to self or others. Different behaviors have varying degrees of risk. A positive risk has more possible positive consequences than a negative one and a negative risk has more possible negative consequences than a positive one. Some

negative consequences are serious. One serious possible negative consequence (e.g., unintended pregnancy or STDs, including HIV) can outweigh any possible positive consequence" (p. 47).

"Reach for Health" Medical Accuracy
There was one medically inaccurate statement in this curriculum:

- "In order to prevent infection, sexually active individuals need to use a latex condom with nonoxynol-9 correctly (every time he/she has sex)" [page cite not provided].

While condoms with the spermicide nonoxynol-9 (N-9) had previously been recommended for reducing the risk of HIV and other STD, this is a serious medical error.
There was also one misleading statement:

- "(Truth or Myth): STDs among teenagers are pretty rare. Myth. 75% of all reported cases of STDs involve people between the ages of 15-30. Thousands of teenagers in the U.S. have STDs. It doesn't matter what age you are; you can become infected if you have unprotected sexual intercourse (without a latex condom) with an infected individual" (p. 64).

In truth, theyrevalence of HPV, chlamydia, and herpes in 15- to 24-year-olds is approximately 14 million.[47] There is also an implication that you can only get STDs from "unprotected" intercourse, which is misleading.

"Reach for Health" Evaluations of Curriculum Effectiveness
There have been several studies relating to the combination of the *Reach for Health* Curriculum and the *Community Youth Service Learning Program*. There has been only one published study (by the authors) on the curriculum alone.
O'Donnell, Stueve, San Doval, et al., 1999.[48]

- Background and Methodology: conducted by curriculum's authors; published in the American Journal of Public Health; originally evaluated in 1994 in two large Brooklyn, NY middle schools (one was "intervention," and the other "control"); same size was 1031 students; in the intervention school, approximately one-half (n=222) were

randomly assigned to receive the "curriculum only," while the remaining (n=255) received both the curriculum and the community youth services.
- Findings:

  - The group receiving both components (the curriculum and the community service) demonstrated a slight impact with regard to frequency of sex over the previous three months.
  - There was no difference in frequency of sex for those who received the curriculum only versus the control group.
  - Students in both interventions showed increased use in "STD protection" and birth control.
  - Sexual activity at 6 month follow-up was higher across the sample, both the study group and the control group.

Curriculum 8: Making Proud Choices

This curriculum is an adaptation and extension of the original *Be Proud! Be Responsible!* curriculum (see review of this curriculum above), adding information on STD and pregnancy prevention and focusing on a younger audience.

"Making Proud Choices" Curriculum Description
Program Authors: L. Jemmott, J. Jemmott III, K. McCaffree, 2001, 2002.

- *Distributed by:* It is published by Select Media, although training is available through ETR Associates.

Format: an eight-module curriculum.

- *Audience:* Developed for middle school adolescents (ages 11-13) and can be delivered in small groups in both a school setting and in youth-serving community- based programs.

Stated Goals/Focus: The curriculum has two stated goals:

  - to give adolescents the tools they need to reduce their risk of sexually transmitted diseases (including HIV) and pregnancy; and

- to allow adolescents to feel comfortable abstaining from sex completely or using condoms if they choose to be sexually active.

"Making Proud Choices" Curriculum Content

Although one of the two main goals of the curriculum is to "allow adolescents to feel comfortable abstaining from sex completely or using condoms", the curriculum only mentions abstinence 18 times, while there are 650 references to condoms. Appendix A lists the content analysis for this and all other curricula reviewed.

Examples of curriculum content:

- "I just want to emphasize that if you have sex, the proud and responsible thing to do is to use condoms" (p. 42).
- "The surest way NOT to get HIV (the virus that causes AIDS) is to practice safer sex" (p. 76).
- "You are right to feel cautious, even a bit afraid, about having sex. You can't look at someone and tell whether or not they have a STD. Take time to get to know a person as a friend before you decide to have sex" (p.. 80).
- "Knowing your sexual partner very well does not mean you are safe. You need to use condoms; then you do not have to worry" (p. 118).
- "Girls who carry condoms are smart, responsible, proud, and safe" (p. 144).
- "Condoms make you feel good about yourself. You know you are safe when you use condoms" (p. 154).
- "Emphasize strategies for how to make condom use more pleasurable. Remember that some of the young people may not be sexually active and that for them, this discussion may not make much sense" (p. 152)
- "The only proud and responsible ways to prevent sexually transmitted disease, like HIV infection, during sexual intercourse from affecting us, our lovers, our families, and our communities is to use latex condoms and encourage everyone we know to do the same" (p. 202).

"Making Proud Choices" Medical Accuracy

There were three medically inaccurate statements in this curriculum. The first two involve an assertion that condoms can prevent HIV infection:

- "How can you prevent HIV/AIDS? By using latex condoms every time you have vaginal intercourse, oral sex or anal sex" (p. 57).

- "The surest way NOT to get HIV (the virus that causes AIDS) is to practice safer sex" (p. 76).

The first statement also does not mention that the FDA has not approved condoms for anal sex. The second statement is not true: the surest way not to sexually acquire HIV is to not have sex.

The third medically inaccurate statement references an incorrect statistic:

- (Q) Are condoms effective? How safe are they? I've heard they aren't safe and fail ten percent of the time, is that true? (A) Latex condoms help protect you from the transmission of HIV and other disease agents. They greatly reduce your risk of infection, and are 95% effective if used properly" (p. 223).

Consistent condom use for penile-vaginal sex can reduce risk of HIV infection by about 85%.

Beyond the above medically inaccurate statements, the curriculum also had a misleading statement:

- *Curriculum statement:* "If used properly, latex condoms are highly effective against most STDs, including HIV" (p. 220).

This statement is misleading: it is unclear what "highly effective" means.

"Making Proud Choices" Evaluation of Curriculum Effectiveness
Jemmott, Jemmott, & Fong, 1998.[49]

- Background and methodology: conducted by curriculum's authors; jublished in the Journal of the American Medical Association; sample size of 659 6' and 7thgrade African-American males and females; no measures of pregnancy or STIs.
- Findings:
  - More effective with sexually experienced youth at baseline; experienced youth in the study group self-reported less sexual intercourse in the previous three months than the control group.
  - Sexually experienced youth at baseline self-reported less incidents of unprotected sex at 3, 6, and 12 month follow-up.

- Study group self-reported more frequent condom use at 3, 6, and 12 months than the control group.
- No delay in sexual initiation was reported.
- No impact on abstinence.

Curriculum 9: Positive Images: Teaching Abstinence, Contraception, and Sexual Health (3rd Edition)

"Positive Images: Teaching Abstinence, Contraception, and Sexual Health" Curriculum Description
Program Authors: P. Brick and B. Taverner, 2001

- *In collaboration with:* Planned Parenthood of Greater Northern New Jersey
- *Funded by:* A grant from Allendale Pharmaceuticals, Inc., makers of "The Today Sponge"
- *Distributed by:* Planned Parenthood.

Format: Twenty-nine, 40-45 minute segments.

- *Audience:* Stated appropriate for high school and college students and (with adaptation) for middle school students. No specific ages mentioned.

Stated Goals/Focus: The primary stated goal of this material is pregnancy prevention, and the secondary goal is the prevention of sexually transmitted infections.

"Positive Images: Teaching Abstinence, Contraception, and Sexual Health" Curriculum Content
Compared with the other curricula reviewed for this study, *Positive Images* mentions abstinence the second most at 87 times *(Reducing the Risk* mentions abstinence 90 times); it mentions marriage more than any other curriculum, at 13 times. Although abstinence is mentioned frequently, the focus of this curriculum is on birth control (as is also evident in the stated goals of the curriculum): forms of birth control are mentioned 987 times. A form of "health" or "healthy" is used 180 times, mostly in reference to healthy

sexuality. Being healthy is closely related to engaging in sexual behaviors with "protection."

Also of note, the curriculum mentions the contraceptive sponge 28 times. Only one other curriculum *(Teen Talk)* mentions the sponge — and that curriculum only mentions the sponge four times. This may be evidence that the funders of the curriculum, who manufacture a contraceptive sponge, have influenced the content.

Of all reviewed curriculum, *Positive Images* had the highest use of "abortion/termination" with 18 *(Teen Talk* was the second highest at 8 mentions) and the "morning after pill" with 24 *(Safer Choices 2* was the second highest at 12 mentions).

Appendix A lists the content analysis for this and all other curricula reviewed.

Examples of curriculum content:

- "Understand that contraception is a way to gain control over one's body, one's life and one's future" (p. x).
- (Students choosing abstinence are told) "Don't leave your abstinence at home, or in your health class, or in your church, synagogue, or mosque. Keep it with you at all times. Pills won't prevent a pregnancy if you forget to take them every day; condoms can't protect you from an STI if they never make it out of a wallet or purse. Abstinence won't work if you don't use it. Take out your 'abstinence' every once in a while and think about it to reaffirm your commitment. Review your reasons for choosing abstinence. How well is it working? What are the strong points? The weak points? ... Decide when and under what circumstance you will cease to abstain (e.g., when you reach a certain age, when you are in a long-term committed relationship or marriage.) ... If you decide abstinence is no longer the right choice for you, you need to choose another method to protect yourself from unwanted pregnancy and STI" (p. 44).
- "What could be done to encourage more people to get Emergency Contraception so they might avoid having to make a decision about an unplanned pregnancy?" (p. 52).
- "A comparison of adolescent sexual behaviors in the United States and other developed countries shows that the rate of sexual intercourse is similar - but the rate of pregnancies and abortions is much higher in the United States. This indicates that under the right conditions, adolescents are able to get and use contraceptives

effectively. What are those conditions? According to the data, the key differences in the other countries are: they have more comprehensive sexuality education, the media provide positive reinforcement for using contraceptives, reproductive health care is more accessible and affordable for teens, and there is less political and social pressure for teens to remain abstinent until marriage. This lesson encourages teens to analyze this data, hypothesize about the differences, and then develop a plan of action" (p. 61).

- "A number of studies demonstrate that Americans greatly exaggerate the health risks of contraceptives and consistently underestimate how well particular methods protect against pregnancy and STIs. Young people have many negative attitudes about contraceptive and safer sex devices. This lesson helps participants overcome such attitudes by creating advertisements for contraceptives and safer sex that are both appealing and accurate, and by developing a public information campaign to encourage condom use" (p. 85).
- "Have volunteers come to the front of the room (preferably an equal number of males and females). Distribute one card to each. Give them a few minutes to arrange themselves in the proper order so their cards illustrate effective condom use from start to finish. Non-participants observe how the group completes this task and review the final order. When the order is correct, post the cards in the front of the room. CORRECT ORDER: (Sexual Arousal, Erection, Leave Room at the Tip, Roll Condom On, Intercourse, Orgasm/Ejaculation, Hold Onto Rim, Withdraw the Penis, Loss of Erection, Relaxation). Ask a volunteer to describe each step in condom use, using the index and middle finger or a model of a penis" (p. 102).

"Positive Images: Teaching Abstinence, Contraception, and Sexual Health (3rd Edition)" Medical Accuracy

There are two inaccurate statements in this curriculum; the first involves condom statistics:

- "Latex condoms are up to 98% effective when used correctly and consistently" (p. 98). Elsewhere, condom effectiveness is listed as between "86% to 97% if used correctly and consistently" (p. xv).

Condom effectiveness rates vary dependent on how one defines condom use. "Perfect use" results in three pregnancies per 100 couples per year[50];

meanwhile, 15% percent of women using condoms for contraception experience an unintended pregnancy during the first year of "typical use,"[51] and 20% of adolescents under the age of 18 using condoms for contraception get pregnant within one year.[52] Consistent condom use for penile-vaginal sex can reduce risk of HIV infection by about 85%.

The second inaccurate statement does not involve medical issues per se, but rather how one can determine if a condom is FDA-approved:

- "Because all condoms marketed in the United States today meet federal quality assurance standards, color, shape and packaging are all a matter of personal preference" (p. 99).

In fact, not all condoms marketed in the United States are FDA approved. In choosing which condom to purchase, the FDA actually states,

- "Always read the label. Look for two things: 1. *The condoms should be made of latex (rubber). ...* [and] ... 2. *The package should say that the condoms are to prevent disease.* If the package doesn't say anything about preventing disease, the condoms may not provide the protection you want, even though they may be the most expensive ones you can buy. Novelty condoms will not say anything about either disease prevention or pregnancy prevention on the package. They are intended only for sexual stimulation, not protection. Condoms which do not cover the entire penis are not labeled for disease prevention and should not be used for this purpose."[53]

Also, the curriculum does not discuss the risks involved with certain types of sexual activity. For example, the curriculum states:

- (Objective) Understand that outercourse (sexual intimacy without intercourse) is a possible option for expressing sexual feelings without risk of pregnancy (p. 11).

While it is true that outercourse does not carry the risk of pregnancy, some sexually transmitted infections (STIs) are transmissible through mutual masturbation. There is fairly strong evidence for the transmission of HPV and herpes via mutual masturbation.[54,55,56,57,58,59,60,61,62,]

Comprehensive Sex Education Curricula   41

"Positive Images: Teaching Abstinence, Contraception, and Sexual Health (3rd Edition)" Evaluation of Curriculum Effectiveness
There have been no evaluations of the effectiveness of this curriculum.

End Notes

[1] Demographic and Behavioral Sciences Branch, NICHD: *Report to the NACHHD Council, 2003,* The National Institute of Child Health and Human Development (NICHD), The Demographic and Behavioral Sciences Branch (DBSB).

[2] The Sexuality Information and Education Council of the United States (SIECUS) has stated that, "Numerous studies and evaluations published in peer-reviewed literature suggest that comprehensive sexuality education is an effective strategy to help young people delay their involvement in sexual intercourse." *[Issues and Answers: Fact Sheet on Sexuality Education,* SIECUS Report, Volume 29, Number 6 - August/September 2001.] Also, with regard to sexually transmitted diseases (STDs), the American Psychological Association has concluded that, "only comprehensive sex education is effective in protecting adolescents from pregnancy and sexually transmitted illnesses at first intercourse and during later sexual activity." [APA Online, American Psychological Association, Press Release, *Based on the Research, Comprehensive Sex Education is more Effective at Stopping the Spread of HIV Infection, Says APA Committee,* http://www.apa.org/releases/sexeducation.html, February 23, 2005.]

[3] These organizations include:
- Sexuality Information and Education Council of the United States (SIECUS), a sexuality education, health, and rights advocacy group;
- ETR (Education, Training, Research) Associates, a publisher of CSE curricula, and their "Resource Center for Adolescent Pregnancy Prevention" (ReCAPP);
- Child Trends, a nonprofit, nonpartisan research organization;
- Planned Parenthood (including national and regional offices);
- The Alan Guttmacher Institute, nonprofit organization focused on sexual and reproductive health research, policy analysis and public education;
- Advocates for Youth, a nonprofit organization dedicated to creating programs and advocating for policies that help young people
- make informed and responsible decisions about their reproductive and sexual health;
- *Emerging Answers: Research Findings on Programs to Reduce Teen Pregnancy,* by Douglas Kirby; and
- Program Archive on Sexuality, Health & Adolescence (PASHA).

[4] *Reach for Health* is often packaged together with *Community Youth Service,* which is a community based program. *Reach for Health* is endorsed as a stand-alone classroom curriculum.

[5] The content analysis counted words used in each curriculum. Of the words counted, variations on the word "condom" occurred 235 times and variations on the word "contraception" occurred 381 times, while variations on the word "abstinence" occurred 87 times.

[6] The three curricula without any medical inaccuracies were *Reducing the Risk, BART = Becoming a Responsible Teen, and Teen Talk.*

[7] Three curricula contain references to nonoxynol-9: see reviews of *Be Proud! Be Responsible!, AIDS Prevention for Adolescents in School, and Reach for Health in Appendix B for more information.*

[8] Twelve peer-reviewed studies that evaluated N-9 were published from 1992 through 2004. None showed any reduction in STDs including HIV; one showed an increase in gonorrhea and two showed increases in HIV.
[9] See review of *Be Proud! Be Responsible!* in Appendix B for more infonnation.
[10] See review of *Safer Choices* in Appendix B for more information.
[11] See review of *Positive Choices* in Appendix B for more information.
[12] See review of *Making Proud Choices* in Appendix B for more information.
[13] *Safer Choices*, Implementation Guide, p. 176.
[14] Trussell J. Contraceptive Efficacy. In Hatcher RA, et al. (Eds.) *ContraceptiveTechnology*. 1998. Chapter 31:779-844, 17th Revised Ed., Ardent Media, New York, NY. As cited in National Institute of Allergy and Infectious Diseases. *Workshop Summaty: Scientific Evidence on Condom Effectiveness for Sexually Transmitted Disease (STD) Prevention*. Bethesda, MD: National Institute of Allergy and Infectious Diseases; 2001.
[15] Trussell J. The essentials of contraception: Efficacy, safety, and personal considerations. In: Hatcher RA, Trussell J, Stewart FH, *et al.*, eds. *Contraceptive Technology*. 18th Revised ed. New York: Ardent Media, Inc.; 2005:221-252.
[16] Grady WR, Hayward MD, Yagi J. Contraceptive failure in the United States: estimates from the 1982 National Survey of Family Growth. *Fam Plann Perspect* 1986;18(5):200-209.
[17] United States House of Representatives, Committee on Government Reform — Minority Staff, Special Investigations Division. (December 2004). "The Content of Federally Funded Abstinence-Only Education Programs." Available at http://reform.democrats
[18] The United States House of Representatives Committee on Government Reform provided a rebuttal to the Waxman report; see United States House of Representatives, Committee on Government Reform. (October 2006). "Abstinence and Its Critics." Available at http://reform.house.gov/UploadedFiles/Abstinence%20and%20its%20Critics.pdf
[19] A third curriculum, *Teen Talk*, showed no impact on initiation of sex overall, but there was a small abstinence effect for males.
[20] Examples of curricula that did show results past 3 months include: (1) *Making Proud Choices* showed positive impacts on increased condom use 6 and 12 months post-intervention; and (2) *Reducing the Risk* showed positive impacts on delaying sexual debut 18 months post intervention.
[21] National Institute of Allergy and Infectious Diseases. *Workshop Summary: Scientific Evidence on Condom Effectiveness for Sexually Transmitted Disease (STD) Prevention*. Bethesda, MD: National Institute of Allergy and Infectious Diseases; 2001.
[22] Kirby D, Barth RP, Leland N et al. Reducing the Risk: impact of a new curriculum on sexual risk-taking. *Family Planning Perspectives* 1991; 23:253-263.
[23] Hubbard BM, Giese ML, Rainey JA. Replication of Reducing the Risk, a Theory-Based Sexuality Curriculum for Adolescents. *Journal of School Health*. 1998;68(6):243-247.
[24] J. Jemmott, L. Jemmott, G. Fong. Reductions in HIV risk-associated sexual behaviors among black male adolescents: effects of an AIDS prevention intervention. *American Journal of Public Health* 1992; 82:372-377.
[25] J. Jemmott, L. Jemmott, G. Fong, K. McCaffree, "Reducing HIV Risk-Associated Sexual Behavior Among Africa American Adolescents: Testing the Generality of Intervention Effects," *American Journal of Community Psychology*, Vol. 27, No. 2, 1999, pp. 161-175.
[26] Trussell J. The essentials of contraception: Efficacy, safety, and personal considerations. In: Hatcher RA, Trussell J, Stewart FH, *et al.*, eds. *Contraceptive Technology*. 18th Revised ed. New York: Ardent Media, Inc.; 2005:221-252.
[27] Grady WR, Hayward MD, Yagi J. Contraceptive failure in the United States: estimates from the 1982 National Survey of Family Growth. *Fam Plann Perspect* 1986;18(5):200-209.
[28] Trussell J. Contraceptive Efficacy. In Hatcher RA, et al. (Eds.) *ContraceptiveTechnology*. 1998. Chapter 31:779-844, 17th Revised Ed., Ardent Media, New York, NY. As cited in National Institute of Allergy and Infectious Diseases. *Workshop Summary: Scientific*

Evidence on Condom Effectiveness for Sexually Transmitted Disease (STD) Prevention. Bethesda, MD: National Institute of Allergy and Infectious Diseases; 2001.

[29] R. A. Hatcher, et al., Contraceptive Technology, 17th revised Edition (New York: Ardent Media, Inc., 1998), p.326.

[30] Trussell J. The essentials of contraception: Efficacy, safety, and personal considerations. In: Hatcher RA, Trussell J, Stewart FH, *et al.,* eds. *Contraceptive Technology.* 18th Revised ed. New York: Ardent Media, Inc.; 2005:221-252.

[31] Grady WR, Hayward MD, Yagi J. Contraceptive failure in the United States: estimates from the 1982 National Survey of Family Growth. *Fam Plann Perspect* 1986;18(5):200-209.

[32] Coyle K, Basen-Engquist K, Kirby D, Parcel G, Banspach S, Collins J, Baumler E, Carvajal S, Harrist R. Safer Choices: Long-term effects of a multi-component school-based HIV, other STD, and pregnancy prevention program—a randomized controlled trial. *Public Health Reports* 2001;116(Suppl 1):82-93.

[33] According to Kirby, Douglas. *Emerging Answers: Researching findings on programs to reduce teen pregnancy.* Washington, DC: National Campaign to Prevent Teen Pregnancy. 2001. pp.115-176

[34] According to ReCAPP (Resource Center for Adolescent Pregnancy Prevention), the Research arm of ETR & Associates, http://www.etr.org/recapp/programs/saferchoices.htm#evaluation

[35] ReCAPP (Resource Center for Adolescent Pregnancy Prevention), the Research arm of ETR & Associates, http://www.ettorg/recapp/programs/saferchoices.htmitevaluation

[36] http://www.socio.com/pasha.htm "PASHA was established by Sociometrics Corporation in 1995, with funding from the US Office of Population Affairs (OPA). The resource is currently funded by the National Institute of Child Health and Human Development (NICHD) and the Centers for Disease Control and Prevention (CDC)."

[37] H. Walter and R. Vaughan. "AIDS risk reduction among a multiethnic sample of urban high school students." *JAMA* 1993; 270:725-730.

[38] Douglas Kirby, *Emerging Answers: Research Findings on Programs to Reduce Teen Pregnancy,* National Campaign to Prevent Teen Pregnancy, Washington, DC., 2001. pp. 115-161.

[39] St. Lawrence, J.S., Brasfield, TL, Jefferson, K.W., Alleyne, E., O'Bannon, R.E., & Shirley, A, Cognitive- Behavioral Intervention To Reduce African-American Adolescents' Risk for HIV Infection. (1995). *Journal of Consulting and Clinical Psychology, 63* (2), 221 - 237

[40] T. McGuinness, M. Mason, G. Tolbert, C.DeFontaine, Becoming Responsible Teens: Promoting the Health of Adolescents in Foster Care Journal of the American Psychiatric Nurses Association, Vol. 8, No. 3, 92-98 (2002).

[41] *Teen Talk: An Adolescent Pregnancy Prevention Program,* Training Manual for Group Discussion Leaders, p. 2., Sociometrics, 2003.

[42] See, for example, http://www.nlm.nih.gov/medlineplusiency/article/002912.htm

[43] Eisen, M., Zellman, G. L., & McAlister, A. L. (1990). Evaluating the impact of a theory-based sexuality and contraceptive education program. *Family Planning Perspectives,* 22(6), 262.

[44] A second study, by Eisen & Zellman (1992), had a sample size of 1,444.

[45] http://www.nichd.nih.gov/about/cpr/dbs/res_reach.htm EDC is included under the supported research category in the National Institute of Child Health and Human Development website. According to the site, "Education Development Center, Inc. (EDC), proposes a study of long-term impact of the Reach for Health (RFH) program of community-based interventions designed to reduce multiple-risk behaviors related to sex, violence, and substance abuse among economically disadvantaged minority youth."

[46] http://www.socio.com/pasha.htm "PASHA was established by Sociometrics Corporation in 1995, with funding from the US Office of Population Affairs (OPA). The resource is currently funded by the National Institute of Child Health and Human Development (NICHD) and the Centers for Disease Control and Prevention (CDC)."

[47] Weinstock H, Berman S, Cates W Jr. Sexually transmitted diseases among American youth: incidence and revalence estimates, 2000. *Perspect Sex Reprod Health.* 2004;36(1):6-10.

[48] O'Donnell L, Stueve A, San Doval, A et al. The effectiveness of the *Reach for Health Community Youth Service* learning program in reducing early and unprotected sex among urban middle school students. *American Journal of Public Health* 1999; 89:176-181.

[49] Jemmott JB, Jemmott LS, Fong GT. Abstinence and safer sex HIV risk-reduction interventions for African American adolescents: a randomized controlled trial. *JAMA* 1998; 279:1529-1536.

[50] Trussell J. Contraceptive Efficacy. In Hatcher RA, et al. (Eds.) *ContraceptiveTechnology*. 1998. Chapter 31:779-844, 17th Revised Ed., Ardent Media, New York, NY. As cited in National Institute of Allergy and Infectious Diseases. *Workshop Summary: Scientific Evidence on Condom Effectiveness for Sexually Transmitted Disease (STD) Prevention*. Bethesda, MD: National Institute of Allergy and Infectious Diseases; 2001.

[51] Trussell J. The essentials of contraception: Efficacy, safety, and personal considerations. In: Hatcher RA, Trussell J, Stewart FH, *et al.*, eds. *Contraceptive Technology*. 18th Revised ed. New York: Ardent Media, Inc.; 2005:221-252.

[52] Grady WR, Hayward MD, Yagi J. Contraceptive failure in the United States: estimates from the 1982 National Survey of Family Growth. *Fam Plann Perspect* 1986;18(5):200-209.

[53] U.S. Food and Drug Administration, Condom Brochure: *Condoms and Sexually Transmitted Diseases ...especially AIDS*. http://www.fda.govioashi/aids/condom.html, Revised July 2005.

[54] Holmes KK, Sparling PF, Mardh P-A, *et al.*, eds. *Sexually Transmitted Diseases*. 3rd ed. New York: McGraw-Hill, Health Professions Division; 1999.

[55] Sonnex C, Strauss S, Gray JJ. Detection of human papillomavirus DNA on the fingers of patients with genital warts. *Sex Transm Infect.* 1999;75(5):317-319.

[56] Frega A, Cenci M, Stentella P, *et al*. Human papillomavirus in virgins and behaviour at risk. *Cancer Lett.* 2003;194(1):21-24.

[57] Ferenczy A, Bergeron C, Richart RM. Human papillomavirus DNA in fomites on objects used for the management of patients with genital human papillomavirus infections. *Obstet Gynecol.* 1989;74(6):950-954.

[58] Bergeron C, Ferenczy A, Richart R. Underwear: contamination by human papillomaviruses. *Am J Obstet Gynecol.* 1990;162(1):25-29.

[59] Strauss S, Sastry P, Sonnex C, Edwards S, Gray J. Contamination of environmental surfaces by genital human papillomaviruses. *Sex Transm Infect.* 2002;78(2):135-138.

[60] Bardell D. Hand-to-hand transmission of herpes simplex virus type 1. *Microbios.* 1989;59:93-100.

[61] Thomas LE 3rd, Sydiskis RJ, DeVore DT, Krywolap GN. Survival of herpes simplex virus and other selected microorganisms on patient charts: potential source of infection. *JAm Dent Assoc.* 1985;111(3):461-464.

[62] Wheeler CE Jr. The herpes simplex problem. *JAm Acad Dermatol.* 1988;18(1 Pt 2):163-168

In: Sexuality Education
Editor: Kelly N. Stanton

ISBN: 978-1-60692-153-1
© 2010 Nova Science Publishers, Inc.

Chapter 2

TEEN PREGNANCY

Centers for Disease Control and Prevention

PUBLIC HEALTH IMPORTANCE

About one-third of girls in the United States get pregnant before age 20. In 2006, a total of 435,427 infants were born to mothers aged 15–19 years, a birth rate of 41.9 per 1,000 women in this age group.[i] More than 80% of these births were unintended, meaning they occurred sooner than desired or were not wanted at any time.[ii] In the United States, rates for pregnancy, birth, sexually transmitted diseases (STDs), and abortion among teenagers are considerably higher than rates in Canada, England, France, Ireland, the Netherlands, Sweden, Japan, and most other developed countries.[iii]

Compared with women who delay childbearing until age 20–21 years, teenaged mothers (aged 19 and younger) are more likely to

- Drop out of high school.
- Be and remain single parents.[iv]

In addition, the children of teenaged mothers are more likely to

- Score lower in math and reading into adolescence.
- Repeat a school grade.
- Be in poor health (as reported by the mother).
- Be taken to emergency rooms for care as infants.
- Be victims of abuse and neglect.
- Be placed in foster care and spend more time in foster care.
- Be incarcerated at some point during adolescence or their early 20s.
- Drop out of high school, give birth as a teenager, and be unemployed or underemployed as a young adult.[3]

These effects remain for the mother and her child even after adjusting for factors that increased the teenager's risk for pregnancy—such as growing up in poverty, having parents with low levels of education, growing up in a single-parent family, and having low attachment to and performance in school.[3]

Teen childbearing costs the United States about $9 billion per year.[v] Although pregnancy and birth rates among girls aged 15–19 years have declined 34% since 1991, birth rates increased for the first time in 2006 (from 40.5 per 1,000 women in this age group in 2005 to 41.9 in 2006).[1] It is too early to tell whether this increase is a trend or a one-time fluctuation in teen birth rates.

WHAT IS CDC DOING?

In 2005, CDC funded a 5-year cooperative agreement with three national organizations, four Title X regional training organizations, and nine state teen pregnancy prevention coalitions. This partnership is designed to increase the capacity of local organizations to select, implement, and evaluate a science-based approach to prevent teen pregnancy, HIV infection, and STDs in their communities. It was built on the successes of a previous 3-year project called Coalition Capacity Building to Prevent Teen Pregnancy. Information on the current cooperative agreement, Promoting Science-based Approaches to Prevent Teen Pregnancy, HIV, and STDs, is available at http://www.cdc.gov/reproductivehealth/AdolescentReproHealth/ScienceAppro ach.htm

WHAT IS A SCIENCE-BASED APPROACH TO TEEN PREGNANCY PREVENTION?

A science-based approach to teen pregnancy prevention can increase a program's chance for success. CDC and external partners collaborated to identify key components for this approach:

- Using demographic, epidemiological and social science research to identify populations at risk of early pregnancy or sexually transmitted diseases, and to identify the risk and protective factors for those populations.
- Using health behavior or health education theory for selecting risk and protective factors that will be addressed by the program, and guide the selection of intervention activities.
- Using a logic model to link risk and protective factors with program strategies and outcomes.
- Selecting, adapting if necessary, and implementing rigorously evaluated programs.
- Conducting process and outcome evaluation of the implemented program, and modifying approach based on results.

ACCOMPLISHMENTS OF CDC-FUNDED PROGRAMS

National, state and regional partners are demonstrating improved capacity to prevent teen pregnancy. A few examples are:

North Carolina

The Adolescent Pregnancy Prevention Coalition of North Carolina (APPCNC) helped Beaufort County successfully apply for state funding to implement a needed primary prevention program in its schools. The Teen Outreach Program has been approved for implementation in a local middle school whose students continue on to a high school with the highest concentration of teen pregnancies in the county. APPCNC supported this program through outreach and education for school officials.

Hawaii

The Hawaii Youth Services Network provides ongoing intensive training and technical assistance to its newly formed coalition of youth-serving organizations, Healthy Youth Hawaii. As a result, all member organizations have adopted or implemented the *Making Proud Choices* curriculum. To date, almost 600 youth have been served. The following activities are under way:

- Parents and Children Together, a family service agency, has implemented *Making Proud Choices* for 7th and 8th graders in an after-school program serving a low-income housing community.
- Planned Parenthood of Hawaii is using *Making Proud Choices* in nine 7th grade classes in one public school.
- The Hakipu'u Learning Center has implemented the curriculum at the Native Hawaiian Charter School with students in grades 9–12.

South Carolina

The South Carolina Campaign to Prevent Teen Pregnancy and the South Carolina Department of Education work together to increase the number of school districts with comprehensive health education teachers who are familiar with science-based approaches and research-proven curricula. This partnership has led to two additional teacher trainings for the *Safer Choices* curriculum. The South Carolina campaign will provide onsite technical assistance to more than 200 teachers on how to implement this program correctly. This partnership has been so successful that the state education department is funding its work.

Teen Pregnancy

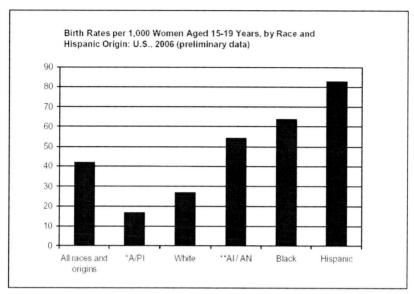

Source: Hamilton BE, Martin JA, Ventura SJ. Births: preliminary data for 2006. Table 3. *National Vital Statistics Reports* 2007;56(7).
*A/PI: Asian/Pacific Islander
**AI/AN: American Indian/Alaska Native

Disparities in Teen Childbearing

Eliminating disparities is an important part of CDC's teen pregnancy prevention work. Several states and regions are working to address the needs of youth at greatest risk for pregnancy and STDs. Teenagers at higher risk include those in foster care and those in some racial/ethnic minority groups, including African Americans, Latinos, Native Americans and Native Hawaiians.

WHAT MORE NEEDS TO BE DONE?

Although teen pregnancy rates have been dropping for several years, this trend appears to be slowing down. CDC will continue to work with partners at federal, state, and local levels to prevent teen pregnancies. Our efforts will include

- Working to eliminate racial, ethnic, and other disparities in teen pregnancy.
- Working to reduce HIV and STD rates among teenagers.
- Applying youth development approaches to promoting adolescent reproductive health.
- Continuing to build state and local capacity to use science-based approaches to promote teen health.

REFERENCES

[i] Hamilton BE, Martin JA, Ventura SJ. Births: preliminary data for 2006. *National Vital Statistics Reports* 2007, 56(7).

[ii] Chandra A, Martinez GM, Mosher WD, Abma JC, Jones J. Fertility, family planning, and reproductive health of U.S. women: data from the 2002 National Survey of Family Growth. *Vital Health Statistics* 2005, 23(25).

[iii] Singh S, Darroch JE. Adolescent pregnancy and childbearing: levels and trends in developed countries. *Family Planning Perspectives* 2000; 32(1), 14-23.

[iv] Maynard RA, editor. *Kids having kids: economic costs and social consequences of teen pregnancy.* Washington, DC: The Urban Institute

Press, 1997.
[v] Hoffman S. By the numbers: the public costs of teen childbearing. Washington, DC: *National Campaign to Prevent Teen Pregnancy*; 2006.

> For more information, please contact
> Centers for Disease Control & Prevention
> Division of Reproductive Health
> National Center for Chronic Disease Prevention & Health Promotion
> 4770 Buford Hwy, NE
> MS K-20
> Atlanta, GA 30341-3717
> Phone: 770-488-5200
> ccdinfo@cdc.gov

CHAPTER SOURCES

The following chapters have been previously published:

Chapter 1 – This is an edited, excerpted and augmented version of The Administration for Children and Famililes (ACF) Department of Health and Human Services (HHS) publication, dated May 2007.

Chapter 2 – This is an edited, excerpted and augmented version of a Centers for Disease Control & Prevention, Division of Reproductive Health, National Center for Chronic Disease Prevention & Health Promotion publication.

INDEX

A

abortion, xii, 8, 29, 30, 38, 45
abstinence, xi, 1, 3, 4, 5, 6, 7, 8, 12, 15, 16, 20, 24, 25, 26, 27, 28, 31, 35, 37, 38, 41, 42
accuracy, xi, 1, 2, 4, 8, 11
ACF, 1, 2, 53
adaptation, 34, 37
adolescence, 46
adolescents, xi, 1, 7, 21, 27, 34, 35, 38, 40, 41, 42, 44
adult, 46
advertisements, 39
advocacy, xi, 1, 3, 41
Africa, 42
African-American, 19, 26, 27, 28, 36, 43, 44, 50
after-school, 26, 48
age, xi, 7, 21, 28, 33, 38, 40, 45, 46
agents, 36
AIDS, 3, 5, 8, 9, 10, 11, 15, 19, 23, 24, 25, 26, 35, 36, 41, 42, 43, 44
Alaska, 49
alcohol, 8, 32
alcohol use, 32
alternatives, 8, 20, 29
American Indian, 49
American Psychological Association (APA), 41
appendix, 15
arousal, 17
assessment, 2
assignment, 13, 20
attachment, 46
attitudes, 22, 39
awareness, 28

B

back, 17
barrier, 30
barriers, 22, 28
BART, 3, 8, 9, 10, 11, 25, 26, 27, 41
behavior, 18, 26, 47
beliefs, 16, 19, 23
benefits, 24, 27, 28
birth, xi, 8, 13, 34, 37, 45, 46
birth control, 8, 13, 34, 37
birth rate, xi, 45, 46
births, xi, 27, 45
blood, 14, 29
boys, 29
Brooklyn, 33

C

Canada, xii, 45
causality, 14
Centers for Disease Control (CDC), 11, 19, 25, 43, 46, 47, 50, 51, 53
childbearing, 46, 50, 51
children, 46
chlamydia, 8, 33
class period, 19

classes, 48
classroom, 15, 25, 26, 41
clinics, 13, 29
coalitions, 46
collaboration, 11, 19, 23, 25, 28, 31, 37
college students, 37
colors, 16
Columbia University, 23
communication, 12, 23
communities, 35, 47
community, 3, 23, 31, 32, 34, 41, 43, 48
community service, 34
components, 3, 4, 34, 47
concentration, 48
conception, 29
condom, 4, 5, 6, 7, 8, 9, 13, 14, 15, 16, 17, 18, 19, 20, 22, 23, 24, 25, 26, 27, 28, 30, 33, 35, 36, 37, 39, 40, 41, 42, 44
contamination, 44
content analysis, 4, 12, 16, 20, 24, 26, 29, 32, 35, 38, 41
contraceptives, 7, 14, 23, 28, 29, 31, 38, 39
control, 8, 13, 14, 19, 33, 34, 36, 37, 38
control group, 14, 19, 34, 36, 37
costs, 46, 50, 51
counseling, 29
couples, 18, 20, 39
covering, 30
curriculum, 2, 3, 4, 6, 7, 11, 12, 13, 14, 15, 16, 17, 18, 19, 20, 21, 22, 23, 24, 25, 26, 27, 28, 29, 30, 31, 32, 33, 34, 35, 36, 37, 38, 39, 40, 41, 42, 48

D

decisions, 15, 23, 41
democrats, 42
Department of Education, 48
Department of Health and Human Services, xi, 1, 53
developed countries, xii, 38, 45, 50
diaphragm, 9, 30
diseases, xi, xii, 1, 14, 34, 41, 43, 45
DNA, 44
doctors, 13

drug use, 32
drugs, 9, 24, 32

E

economically disadvantaged, 43
education, 1, vii, xi, 1, 3, 4, 7, 31, 41, 42, 43, 48
ejaculation, 30
England, xii, 45
ethnic minority, 50
evening, 13
excuse, 5
exposure, 22
eyes, 26

F

failure, 6, 8, 13, 18, 21, 24, 25, 27, 42, 43, 44
family, 13, 46, 48, 50
family planning, 13, 50
FDA, 6, 18, 36, 40
feelings, 32, 40
females, 5, 7, 19, 27, 31, 36, 39
film, 10
focusing, 34
Food and Drug Administration, 44
France, xii, 45
funding, 15, 31, 43, 48
funds, 15

G

gender, 27
genital warts, 9, 44
girls, xi, 29, 45, 46
goals, 2, 15, 23, 26, 34, 35, 37
gonorrhea, 9, 14, 42
government, viii
grades, 14, 48
groups, xi, 1, 3, 19, 34, 50

H

hands, 32
Hawaii, 48
health, 9, 11, 31, 37, 38, 39, 41, 46, 47, 48, 50
Health and Human Services (HHS), 1, 53
health care, 39
health education, 11, 47, 48
herpes, 33, 40, 44
herpes simplex, 44
herpes simplex virus type 1, 44
high risk, 24, 25, 27
high school, 12, 15, 20, 23, 28, 37, 43, 46, 48
HIV, 3, 6, 9, 11, 12, 13, 14, 15, 16, 17, 18, 19, 20, 21, 22, 23, 24, 26, 28, 32, 33, 34, 35, 36, 40, 41, 42, 43, 44, 46, 50
homework, 20
House, 42
housing, 48
HPV, 33, 40
human, 44
human papillomavirus, 44

I

IDS, 11
implementation, 22, 48
incidence, 43
income, 48
Indian, 49
infancy, 29
infants, xi, 45, 46
infection, 12, 16, 20, 24, 32, 33, 35, 36, 40, 44, 46
infections, xi, 1, 21, 37, 40, 44
initiation, 7, 14, 15, 22, 25, 27, 31, 37, 42
injury, viii
insight, 4
intervention, 15, 22, 31, 33, 42, 47
intimacy, 32, 40
Investigations, 42
Ireland, xii, 45

J

JAMA, 25, 43, 44
Japan, xii, 45
Jefferson, 43
junior high, 15, 28

K

killing, 30

L

language, 18
latex, 6, 13, 21, 22, 27, 33, 35, 36, 40
Latinos, 50
learning, 17, 31, 44
limitations, 7
long-term impact, 43
love, 9
low-income, 48
lubrication, 17

M

males, 5, 16, 18, 19, 27, 31, 36, 39, 42
management, 44
market, 20
marriage, 6, 7, 8, 9, 24, 37, 38, 39
measures, 27, 30, 36
media, 39
men, 17
microorganisms, 44
middle schools, 33
minority, 31, 43, 50
minority groups, 50
mirror, 2, 4
misleading, 6, 21, 30, 33, 36
misleading statements, 6, 21, 30
morning, 9, 38
mothers, xi, 45, 46
motivation, 20

N

National Institutes of Health (NIH), xi, 1, 14
Native American, 50
Native Hawaiian, 48, 50
needles, 24
negative attitudes, 39
negative consequences, 32
neglect, 46
negotiation, 9, 26
Netherlands, xii, 45
New Jersey, 4, 15, 37
New York, 15, 23, 42, 43, 44
North Carolina, 48

O

organ, 17
orgasm, 9, 17, 29
orientation, 10

P

Pacific Islander, 49
packaging, 40
parenthood, 9
parents, 9, 23, 29, 46
partnership, 46, 48
paternity, 28
patients, 44
peer, 7, 22, 41, 42
pelvis, 17
penis, 6, 17, 30, 39, 40
personal values, 23, 24
phone, 32
planning, 13, 50
plastic, 30
play, 16, 17, 29
pleasure, 9, 16, 29
policymakers, xi, 1
poor, 46
poor health, 46
population, 26
positive attitudes, 22
positive reinforcement, 39
poverty, 46
preference, 40
pregnancy, xi, 1, 2, 6, 10, 12, 14, 16, 18, 19, 20, 21, 22, 24, 28, 29, 30, 32, 33, 34, 36, 37, 38, 39, 40, 41, 43, 45, 46, 47, 50
pregnancy test, 29
pregnant, xi, 7, 10, 21, 22, 28, 29, 40, 45
pressure, 39
prevention, 16, 21, 23, 24, 34, 37, 40, 42, 43, 46, 47, 48, 50
private, 28
probability, 28
prognosis, 23
program, 3, 15, 23, 26, 32, 41, 43, 44, 47, 48
property, viii
protection, 9, 10, 12, 13, 17, 20, 22, 34, 38, 40
protective factors, 47
public, 39, 41, 48, 51
public education, 41
publishers, 2

Q

quality assurance, 40

R

R&D, 19
rape, 10
reading, 46
reinforcement, 39
relationship, 5, 8, 38
relationships, 24, 25
reproduction, 10
research design, 7
reservoir, 13, 30
resources, 3, 5, 23
rings, 26
risk, 6, 9, 10, 14, 15, 16, 18, 21, 23, 24, 25, 26, 27, 30, 32, 33, 34, 36, 40, 42, 43, 44, 46, 47, 50

Index

risk behaviors, 43
risk factors, 23
risks, 4, 5, 6, 8, 10, 12, 16, 26, 28, 30, 31, 32, 39, 40
risk-taking, 42
rubber, 6, 10, 18, 40
rubbers, 29

S

safety, 42, 43, 44
sample, 7, 14, 15, 18, 19, 27, 31, 34, 36, 43
school, 3, 12, 15, 20, 22, 23, 26, 28, 33, 34, 37, 43, 44, 46, 48
search, 2
secretion, 14
selecting, 47
self-efficacy, 19, 21, 22
self-report, 36, 37
semen, 14, 30
sensations, 29
series, 25
services, viii, 34
sex, 2, 3, 5, 6, 7, 8, 9, 10, 12, 13, 14, 15, 16, 17, 18, 20, 21, 22, 24, 25, 27, 29, 33, 34, 35, 36, 39, 40, 41, 42, 43, 44
sexual activities, 26
sexual activity, xi, 1, 2, 4, 5, 8, 12, 26, 28, 32, 40, 41
sexual behavior, 18, 19, 32, 38, 42
sexual health, 41
sexual intercourse, 8, 12, 20, 23, 24, 25, 32, 33, 35, 36, 38, 41
sexual orientation, 10
sexual violence, 32
sexuality, 3, 5, 10, 38, 39, 41, 43
sexually transmitted disease(s) (STD), xi, xii, 1, 2, 3, 6, 10, 11, 12, 13, 14, 18, 20, 21, 22, 24, 30, 33, 34, 35, 41, 42, 43, 44, 45, 47, 50
sexually transmitted infections (STIs), xi, 1, 27, 32, 36, 37, 38, 39, 40
shape, 40
shoulders, 32
sibling, 5, 24

skills, 10, 12, 20, 26
social consequences, 50
South Carolina, 48
sperm, 20, 30
spermicide, 4, 6, 10, 17, 18, 24, 33
stages, 32
standards, 6, 40
statistics, 6, 7, 39
strategies, 35, 47
strength, 3
strokes, 17
students, 12, 13, 15, 18, 20, 22, 23, 26, 28, 30, 33, 37, 43, 44, 48
subgroups, 14
substance abuse, 43
suspects, 29
Sweden, xii, 45
syphilis, 10

T

tactics, 10
teacher training, 48
teachers, 48
teaching, xi, 1, 26
technical assistance, 48
teenagers, xii, 12, 28, 29, 33, 45, 50
teens, xi, 1, 2, 20, 39
Texas, 19, 28
training, 26, 28, 34, 46, 48
transmission, 2, 18, 20, 23, 24, 25, 36, 40, 44
trial, 43, 44

U

United States, xi, 6, 38, 40, 41, 42, 43, 44, 45, 46
urine, 29

V

vagina, 17, 18, 30
values, 23, 24

venereal disease, 11
victims, 46
violence, 32, 43
virus, 24, 25, 35, 36, 44
visualization, 26
vulva, 18

warts, 9, 44
water, 27
wear, 5, 24
withdrawal, 11
women, xi, 7, 17, 21, 40, 45, 46, 50
worry, 17, 35

W

walking, 26

Y

young women, 17